D0116787

Eyewitness
ROCKS &
MINERALS

Slice from
septarian nodule

Garnet-chlorite schist

Cinnabar

Hematite

Gypsum desert rose

Granite

Wenlock limestone
with triolobite fossils

Opal

Eyewitness
ROCKS &
MINERALS

Cut
tourmalines

Written by
Dr. R. F. SYMES
and the staff of the
Natural History Museum,
London

Geothite

Pyrite

Obsidian

Sulfur

Nephrite
"tiki"

Labradorite

DK Publishing

Magnifying lens

DK

LONDON, NEW YORK,
MELBOURNE, MUNICH, and DELHI

Project editor Janice Lacock
Art editor Neville Graham
Managing art editor Jane Owen
Special photography Colin Keates (Natual History
Museum, London) and Andreas Einsiedel
Editorial consultants
Dr. R.F. Symes (Natural History Museum, London)
and Dr. Wendy Kirk (University College London)

REVISED EDITION
Managing editors Andrew Macintyre, Camilla Hallinan
Managing art editors Jane Thomas, Martin Wilson
Editors Angela Wilkes, Sue Nicholson
Art editor Catherine Goldsmith
Production Jenny Jacoby, Georgina Hayworth
Picture research Angela Anderson, Claire Bowers, Kate Lockley
DTP designers Siu Chan, Andy Hilliard, Ronaldo Julien
U.S. editor Elizabeth Hester
Senior editor Beth Sutinis
Art director Dirk Kaufman
U.S. production Chris Avgherinos
U.S. DTP designer Milos Orlovic

This Eyewitness ® Guide has been conceived by
Dorling Kindersley Limited and Editions Gallimard

This edition published in 2011
First published in the United States in 2008
by DK Publishing, 375 Hudson Street, New York, New York 10014

A catalog record for this book is available from the Library of Congress.
ISBN 978-0-7566-9696-2

Color reproduction by Colourscan, Singapore
Manufactured in USA by Worzalla

Discover more at
www.dk.com

Mixed rough
and polished
pebbles

Chisel

Geologist's hammer

Chalcedony cameo

Contents

Cut citrine

Baryte desert rose

Clear topaz

Cut amethyst

The Earth

Early view of Earth with a central fire

ONE OF THE NINE planets that revolve around the Sun, the Earth is thought to be about 4.6 billion years old. Geology is the study of the history of the Earth. Because rocks can provide valuable information about the Earth in previous times, geologists study them and work out the processes and events that produced them. Since humans can currently bore only a few miles into the crust, we cannot sample rocks from the mantle directly. The rocks and minerals shown here come from a wide range of environments, and introduce important features that are explained in more detail later in the book.

PRECIOUS METALS
Platinum, silver, and gold are valuable and rare metals. *For more information, see pp. 58–59.*

SEASHORE PEBBLES
These are formed by the weathering of larger rocks by wave action. *For more information, see pp. 14–15.*

Gold in quartz vein

CRYSTAL HABITS
The shape of a crystal is known as its habit. *For more information, see pp. 46–47.*

Cubes of pyrite

MINERAL ORES
These are the source of most useful metals. *For more information, see pp. 56–57.*

THE STRUCTURE OF THE EARTH
The Earth consists of three major parts: the core, the mantle, and the crust. The crust and upper mantle form continental and oceanic "plates" that move slowly over the mantle beneath. The closer to the center of the Earth, the greater the temperature and pressure.

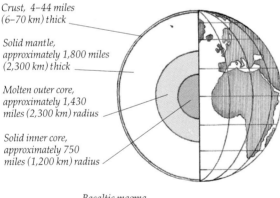

Crust, 4–44 miles (6–70 km) thick

Solid mantle, approximately 1,800 miles (2,300 km) thick

Molten outer core, approximately 1,430 miles (2,300 km) radius

Solid inner core, approximately 750 miles (1,200 km) radius

Cut citrine, a variety of quartz

Cassiterite (tin ore) from Bolivia

Diamond in kimberlite

GEMSTONES
Rare, durable, and attractive minerals may be cut as gemstones. They are mainly used in jewelry. *For more information, see pp. 50–55.*

Quartz crystals from France

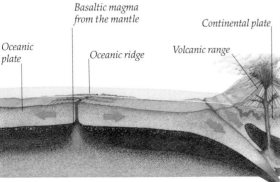

Basaltic magma from the mantle

Continental plate

Oceanic ridge

Volcanic range

Oceanic plate

MOVING PLATES
Where plates collide, mountain ranges like the Himalayas may form. In the ocean, material from the mantle fills the gap between plates to form a ridge. In other areas, oceanic plates are forced down beneath continental plates, causing volcanic activity.

CRYSTALS
Many minerals form regular-shaped solids with flat surfaces, known as crystals. *For more information, see pp. 44–47.*

Shelly limestone

FOSSILS
These rocks contain the remains of, or impressions made by, former plants or animals. *For more information, see pp. 38–39.*

Quartzite
beach
pebbles

IGNEOUS ROCKS
The most common types
of rocks have formed
from molten magma.
*For more information,
see pp. 16–17.*

Granite

Delta

Suez Canal

City of Cairo

Nile River

**SATELLITE PICTURE OF
NILE RIVER AND DELTA**
The Nile River carries
rock debris eroded from
rocks in central Egypt
and deposits it in the
delta and sea, where it
may eventually form
sedimentary rocks
(pp. 11 and 20).

VOLCANIC ROCKS
Volcanic activity
produces a number
of different types of
rocks and lava. *For more
information, see pp. 18–19.*

Hawaiian
ropy lava

Carboniferous
Limestone

*Ingito Hills on edge of East
African Rift Valley*

Lake Amboseli, a dry lake

Chyulu mountain range, Kenya

SEDIMENTARY ROCKS
This group of rocks is formed
by the accumulation and
compaction of loose
sediments that have
built up in layers.
*For more information,
see pp. 20–23.*

Anthracite, the
hardest form of coal

Mount Meru

*Mount
Kilimanjaro*

*Pangani
River valley*

*Glaciers
of Kibo*

COAL
Coal is a sedimentary rock and has formed
from the fossilized remains of plants. *For
more information, see pp. 36–37.*

SATELLITE PICTURE OF EAST AFRICA
This area shows a range of landscapes, formed from different
rocks: for example, volcanic rocks (p. 18) forming volcanic
Mount Kilimanjaro, and evaporites (p. 21) in dried-up lakes.

What are rocks and minerals?

ROCKS ARE NATURAL AGGREGATES or combinations of one or more minerals. Some rocks, such as quartzite (pure quartz) and marble (pure calcite) contain only one mineral. Most, however, consist of more than one kind. Minerals are naturally occurring inorganic solids with definite chemical compositions and an ordered atomic arrangement. Here, two common rocks—granite and basalt—are shown along with individual specimens of the major minerals of which they are formed. Rock-forming minerals can be divided into several groups—these are described in more detail on pages 42–43.

James Hutton (1726–97), one of the founders of modern geology

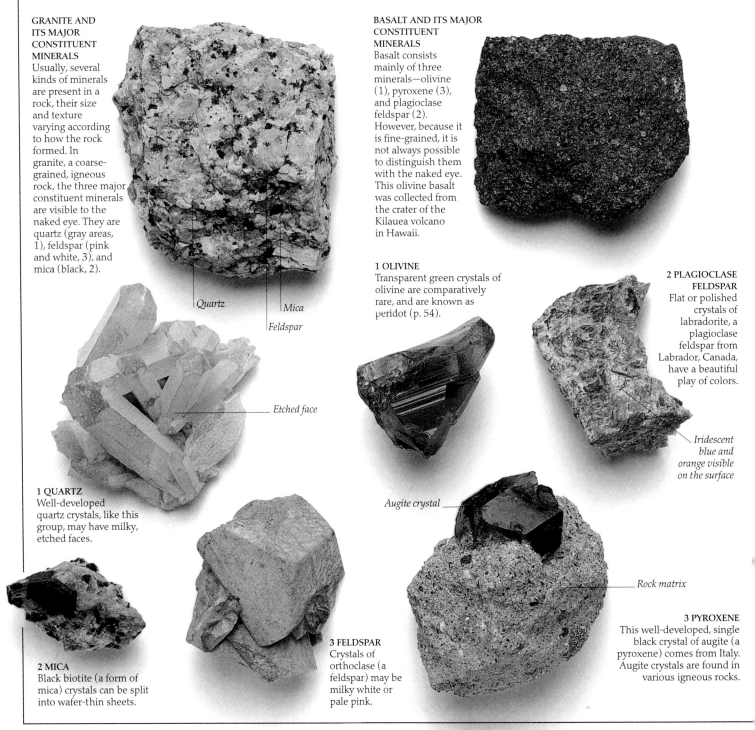

GRANITE AND ITS MAJOR CONSTITUENT MINERALS
Usually, several kinds of minerals are present in a rock, their size and texture varying according to how the rock formed. In granite, a coarse-grained, igneous rock, the three major constituent minerals are visible to the naked eye. They are quartz (gray areas, 1), feldspar (pink and white, 3), and mica (black, 2).

Quartz

Mica

Feldspar

BASALT AND ITS MAJOR CONSTITUENT MINERALS
Basalt consists mainly of three minerals—olivine (1), pyroxene (3), and plagioclase feldspar (2). However, because it is fine-grained, it is not always possible to distinguish them with the naked eye. This olivine basalt was collected from the crater of the Kilauea volcano in Hawaii.

1 OLIVINE
Transparent green crystals of olivine are comparatively rare, and are known as peridot (p. 54).

2 PLAGIOCLASE FELDSPAR
Flat or polished crystals of labradorite, a plagioclase feldspar from Labrador, Canada, have a beautiful play of colors.

Iridescent blue and orange visible on the surface

Etched face

1 QUARTZ
Well-developed quartz crystals, like this group, may have milky, etched faces.

Augite crystal

Rock matrix

3 PYROXENE
This well-developed, single black crystal of augite (a pyroxene) comes from Italy. Augite crystals are found in various igneous rocks.

3 FELDSPAR
Crystals of orthoclase (a feldspar) may be milky white or pale pink.

2 MICA
Black biotite (a form of mica) crystals can be split into wafer-thin sheets.

The scope of rock forms

Rocks and minerals occur in many diverse forms. Rocks do not necessarily have to be hard and resistant—loose sand and wet clay are also considered rocks. The individual size of minerals in a rock ranges from a fraction of an inch in a fine-grained volcanic rock to several yards in a granite pegmatite.

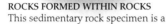

ROCKS FORMED WITHIN ROCKS
This sedimentary rock specimen is a claystone septarian nodule. Nodules such as this are formed when groundwater redistributes minerals within a rock in a particular pattern. Nodules are sometimes known as "concretions." Here, calcite forms the pattern of veins.

CRYSTALS OF ORE MINERAL
Orange red tabular crystals of the mineral wulfenite from Arizona are formed in veins that carry lead and molybdenum.

Eruption of Mount Pelée, Martinique, on August 5, 1851

ROCKS FROM VOLCANIC ERUPTION
Despite its extraordinary appearance, "Pele's hair" is technically a rock. It consists of golden brown hairlike fibers of basalt glass that occasionally enclose minute olivine crystals. It was formed from the eruption of basaltic magma as a lava spray.

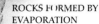

ROCKS FORMED BY EVAPORATION
Stalactites are formed from substances that are deposited when dripping water evaporates (p. 22).
This spectacular blue green stalactite is composed entirely of the mineral chalcanthite (copper sulfate). It formed from copper-rich waters in a mine.

Section of a mine roof colored with deposits of the copper mineral, chalcanthite

Lighter bands of pyroxene and plagioclase feldspar

Dark layer of chromite

ROCKS THAT FORM IN LAYERS
Norite is an igneous rock composed of the minerals pyroxene, plagioclase feldspar, and the chromium-rich mineral chromite. In this specimen from South Africa, the dark and light minerals have separated from each other so that the rock is layered. The dark chromite layers are an important source of chromium.

How rocks are formed

GEOLOGICAL PROCESSES work in constant cycles—redistributing the chemical elements, minerals, and rocks within and at the surface of the Earth. The processes that occur within the Earth, such as metamorphism and mountain building, are driven by the Earth's internal heat. Surface processes, such as weathering, are activated by the Sun's energy.

VOLCANIC ACTIVITY
When rocks of the crust and upper mantle melt, they form magma that may be extruded (forced out) at the Earth's surface by volcanic activity. The resulting rocks are extrusive igneous rocks (p. 16). The most common example is basalt.

Basaltic lava from a lava flow in Hawaii

Gabbro, the coarse-grained equivalent of basalt, from Finland

Andesite formed from a volcanic eruption in the Solomon Islands in the Pacific

Pure quartz sand formed from weathered granites or sandstones

VOLCANIC LANDMARK
Le Puy de Dôme, France, is a plug that was once the central core of an ancient volcano.

IGNEOUS INSELBERG
Sugar Loaf Mountain, Brazil, consists of intrusive igneous rocks that have eventually reached the surface when rocks covering them were weathered away.

Volcanic activity

Weathering

Surface

Igneous rocks

Melting

Magma

Migmatite from Finland

Feldspar crystal

Granite, containing large rectangular crystals of pink feldspar, from northern England

MELTING *right*
Occasionally, high temperatures and pressures cause rocks to partially melt. If the rock is then squeezed, snakelike veins may form. Migmatites are mixed rocks consisting of a metamorphic "host," such as gneiss or schist, cut by veins of granite. They demonstrate the passage of rocks from the metamorphic state to the molten or igneous state.

ROCKS FROM MAGMA
Rocks formed within the Earth from molten magma are called intrusive igneous rocks (p. 16). Those that cooled slowly, deep under the surface, are described as plutonic, after Pluto, the Greek god of the underworld. One such rock, granite, can form enormous masses called batholiths in mountain belts.

WEATHERING
As the weather acts on rocks it may lead to chemical changes or cause the rocks to fragment (p. 12) and to form sediments. For example, sand grains are produced when quartz-bearing rocks are broken down, and clays form from weathered rocks full of feldspar.

Clays produced by weathering become important parts of soils

RIVER TRANSIT
Rivers such as these (seen from space) carry rock fragments from one area to another. The Mississippi alone deposits thousands of tons of debris into its delta each day.

DEPOSITION OF SEDIMENTS
Sediments are transported by rivers, or by the wind in desert regions. When the wind or water slows down, as when a river runs into a lake, the sediment is deposited into layers of different sized particles. When these are compacted (pressed) together, they form sedimentary rocks (p. 20).

Layered sandstone from Arkansas

Banded claystone from Uganda

200-million-year-old desert sandstone from Scotland

THE ROCK CYCLE
There is no starting point in this cycle that has been going on for millions of years.

Transport

Deposition

Heat and pressure

Sedimentary rocks

Metamorphic rocks

METAMORPHIC ROCKS
Quartz veins stand out in this schist rock face in Scotland. The area contains many metamorphic rocks.

Quartzite, an altered sandstone, formed by pressure and heat beneath the Earth's surface

Granite

Gneiss

Gneiss, a banded metamorphic rock

Mica schist formed from metamorphosed claystones

METAMORPHISM
The deeper a rock is within the Earth, the greater the pressure exerted on it from the rocks above it, and the higher the temperature. Pressure and heat cause the rocks to change or "metamorphose" as the minerals recrystallize. The new rocks are called metamorphic rocks (p. 24).

11

Weathering and erosion

ALL ROCKS BREAK DOWN at the Earth's surface. When rocks break down without movement (as they stand) this is called weathering. Weathering can be chemical or mechanical. When weathered rocks break down as they are moved—by the action of water, ice, or the wind—this is called erosion.

Wind erosion

Constant attack by sediment-laden wind may slowly grind away at a rock and erode it.

MONUMENT VALLEY, ARIZONA.
Large-scale abrasion by the wind produces huge, protruding landforms called buttes.

ABRASION BY THE WIND
The abrasive action of the wind wears away softer layers of rock and leaves the harder ones sticking out, as in this desert rock from Somalia.

SAND BLASTING
Faceted desert pebbles, formed by sand constantly being blown against them, are called dreikanters.

Weathering caused by temperature fluctuations

Rock expands and contracts as the temperature changes, causing it to break up. Frost shattering may also be caused when water in the rock freezes and expands.

Sandstone composed of sand accumulated 200 million years ago in a desert environment

Sand from a present-day desert in Saudi Arabia

DESERT EROSION
Rocks formed in desert conditions, where sediment is carried by wind, are often reddish in color and composed of characteristically rounded sand grains.

DESERT ENVIRONMENT
Wind and temperature changes cause continual weathering and bizarre, barren landscapes in the Sahara Desert.

ONION-SKIN WEATHERING
In this type of weathering, changes in temperature cause the surface layers of rock to expand, contract, and finally peel away from the underlying rock.

Fine-grained dolerite

Onion-skin weathered dolerite

Peeling layers, like onion skins, caused by changes in temperature

Chemical weathering

Only a few minerals can resist weathering by acidic rainwater. Minerals dissolved at the surface may be carried downward and redeposited into the soil and rock below.

Fresh, unaltered granite

Coarse, weathered granite

GRANITE TORS
Tors, weathered rounded rocks, are formed from the remnants left when the surrounding rocks have been eroded away. This example is on Dartmoor, England.

ALTERED MINERALS
Granite is split by the expansion of water as it freezes. Its constituent minerals are then chemically altered, producing coarse rock fragments.

Rock altered by groundwater

Secondary minerals

CHEMICAL CHANGES
Chemical weathering of an ore vein may cause redistribution of minerals. The bright colored minerals were formed from deposits of minerals that dissolved from weathered rocks at higher levels. They are called secondary deposits.

TROPICAL WEATHERING
In certain tropical climates, quartz is dissolved and carried away, while feldspars are altered to clay minerals that may accumulate on the surface as a thick deposit of bauxite (p. 56).

Ice erosion

As glaciers move they pick up fragments of rock that become frozen into the base of the ice. The moving, frozen mass causes further erosion of underlying rocks.

PARTHENON, ATHENS, GREECE
Chemicals in the air can react with stone and cause drastic weathering. This can be seen on the Parthenon and on gargoyles on buildings.

Large rock fragment

Scratches caused by a glacier

SCRATCHED ROCK
The deep gouge marks on this limestone from Grindelwald, Switzerland, were caused by abrasive rock fragments contained in the glacier that flowed over it.

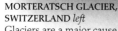

MORTERATSCH GLACIER, SWITZERLAND *left*
Glaciers are a major cause of erosion in mountainous regions.

GLACIER DEPOSITS
A till is a deposit left by a melting glacier, and contains crushed rock fragments ranging from microscopic grains to large pebbles. Ancient tills that have become packed into hard rock are called tillite. This specimen is from the Flinders Range in South Australia that was covered with glaciers some 600 million years ago.

Rocks on the seashore

AT THE SEASHORE, geological processes can be seen taking place. Many seashores are backed by cliffs, beneath which is a deposit of coarse material that has fallen from above. This is gradually broken up by the sea, and sorted into pebbles, gravel, sand, and mud. Then the various sizes of sediment are deposited separately—this is the raw material for future sedimentary rocks (p. 20).

Pebbles on Chesil Beach, England

GRADED GRAINS
On the beach, these pebbles are sorted by wave and tide action. The sand is pure quartz, the other rock-forming minerals were washed away by constant wave movement.

Large, coarse pebbles

SKIPPING STONES
As every schoolchild knows, the best stones for skipping are disk-shaped. They are most likely to be sedimentary or metamorphic rocks, since these split easily into sheets.

Mica schist

Irregularly shaped pyrite nodule

Slates

HIDDEN CRYSTALS
Pyrite nodules are common in chalk areas. They may develop interesting shapes. The dull outside breaks to reveal unexpected, radiating crystals inside.

LOCAL STONES
These pebbles reflect the local geology, all coming from the rocks of the immediate neighborhood of the beach where they were collected. They are metamorphic rocks that have been worn into flat disks.

SHELLY PEBBLES
Uninhabited sea shells are subjected to continuous wave action. In time, the sharp edges of broken shells may become smoothed and form pebbles. These are from a beach in New Zealand.

AMBER PEBBLES
Amber is the fossil resin of extinct coniferous trees that lived thousands of years ago. It is especially common along the Baltic coasts of Russia and Poland.

PRESERVED WAVES
Ripple marks and other similar structures form underwater from sand carried by currents, and can be seen on many beaches at low tide. In this specimen from Finland, ripple marks are preserved in sandstone, showing that the same sedimentary processes have been going on for millions of years (p. 20).

BLACK SANDS

In areas of volcanic activity, beach sand may contain dark minerals and often no quartz. The olivine sand comes from Raasay, Scotland, while the magnetite-bearing sand is from Tenerife, an island off the northwest coast of Africa.

Dark olivine sand

Magnetite-bearing sand

Black volcanic ash beach on north coast of Santorini, Greece

Medium-size, coarse pebbles

Small, fine pebbles

Finest pebbles

Quartz sand

DISCOVERED IN CHALK
Because flint nodules are hard, they resist abrasion (scraping) and so may be seen on beaches in Chalk areas, such as those below the famous White Cliffs of Dover, England.

Chalk cliffs often produce pyrite and flint nodules

Nodule of marcasite with nobbly exterior

Interior of marcasite reveals glistening crystals radiating outward

Flint nodules from below Chalk cliffs

GRANITIC ORIGIN
In granite country, beach pebbles tend to be of quartz (an abundant vein mineral) or pink or gray granite.

FOREIGN MATERIAL
Not all beach rocks are from local areas. This porphyritic igneous rock was probably carried across the North Sea from Norway to England by ice during the last Ice Age.

Assorted glass pebbles

Brick pebble

SYNTHETIC PEBBLES
Aside from the usual natural minerals and rocks, man-made objects may be washed ashore, possibly from ships', or dumped on the beach. Some of them may eventually become rounded by wave action.

PROTECTING THE BEACH
Man-made jetties keep pebbles and sand from drifting.

Igneous rocks

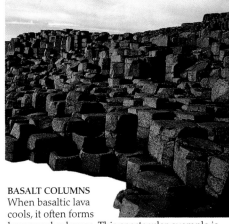

THESE **ROCKS** are formed when molten magma from deep within the Earth's crust and upper mantle (p. 6) cools and solidifies. There are two types: intrusive and extrusive. Intrusive rocks solidify within the Earth's crust and only appear at the surface after the rocks above them have eroded away. Extrusive rocks are formed when magma erupts from a volcano as lava, then cools at the surface.

Basalt needle, St. Helena

BASALT COLUMNS
When basaltic lava cools, it often forms hexagonal columns. This spectacular example is the Giant's Causeway in Northern Ireland.

Biotite granite

Graphic granite

Red granite

Black grains are biotite, a form of mica (p. 42)

Long, angular quartz crystals look like ancient writing against the larger pale pink feldspar crystals

GRANITE
A very common intrusive rock, granite consists mainly of coarse grains of quartz, feldspar, and mica (p. 8). The individual grains are large because they formed as the magma cooled slowly deep in the earth. Granite is usually speckled and varies in color from gray to red according to the different amounts of constituent minerals. Granite is found in many parts of the world. The biotite granite shown here comes from Hay Tor, an outcrop at the highest point on Dartmoor in southwest England (p. 13).

Red coloring due to the high level of potassium feldspar in the rock

PITCHSTONE
Formed when volcanic lava cools very quickly, pitchstone contains some small crystals of feldspar and quartz and has a dull, resinlike appearance. Pitchstone may be brown, black or gray, and large crystals of feldspar and quartz are sometimes visible.

OBSIDIAN
Like pitchstone, obsidian is a glass formed from rapidly cooled lava. It forms so quickly that there is no time for crystals to grow. The sharp edges shown on this sample from Iceland are characteristic of obsidian, hence its use as an early tool (p. 29).

Phenocryst of feldspar

FELDSPAR PORPHYRY
Porphyries are rocks that contain large crystals called phenocrysts within a medium-grained rock. This particular sample contains feldspar crystals and comes from Wales.

Olivine

Pyroxene

Plagioclase feldspar

GABBRO
An intrusive rock, gabbro consists of dark minerals such as olivine and augite. It has coarse grains, since large crystals formed when the magma slowly cooled. This sample is from the Isle of Skye, Scotland.

THIN SECTION OF GABBRO
When a very thin slice of rock is viewed under a microscope using a particular kind of light, hidden features, such as crystal shape, are revealed (p. 42). Here, the dark minerals are olivine and augite. The light-colored mineral is plagioclase feldspar.

BASALT
Formed from hardened lava, basalt is the most common extrusive rock. It is similar in composition to gabbro but has finer grains. When the lava cools, it may split into many-sided columns. Among the most well known of these spectacular structures are The Needle on St. Helena, an island in the Atlantic and the Giant's Causeway in Northern Ireland.

Vesicular basalt

Empty vesicles or holes

Amygdaloidal basalt

Hole filled with calcite

VESICULAR VOLCANIC ROCKS
Both rocks are basalts that were formed when bubbles of gas were trapped in hot lava scum. The vesicular basalt is light and full of holes known as vesicles. In amygdaloidal basalt, the holes were later filled in with minerals such as calcite. These rocks were collected from Hawaii, an area of great volcanic activity.

PERIDOTITE
A dark, heavy rock mainly containing minerals called olivine and pyroxene, peridotite is presumed to lie under layers of gabbro 6 miles (10 km) beneath the ocean floor. This sample was found in Odenwald, Germany.

Green olivine crystals

Dark pyroxene crystals

Calcite vein

SERPENTINITE
As its name suggests, the dominant mineral in this coarse-grained red and green rock is serpentine. It is streaked with white veins of calcite. Serpentinite is common in the Alps.

Volcanic rocks

ROCKS THAT ARE FORMED by volcanic activity can be divided into two groups: pyroclastic rocks, and acid and basic lavas. Pyroclastic rocks are formed from either solid rock fragments or bombs of lava blown out of the throat of a volcano. The bombs solidify as they fly through the air. Rocks formed from hardened lavas vary according to the type of lava. Acid lavas are thick and sticky, flow very slowly and form steep-sided volcanoes. The more fluid, basic lavas form flatter volcanoes or may well up through cracks in the seafloor. Basic lavas are fast-flowing and so quickly spread out to cover vast areas.

Ejection of lava from Eldfell, Iceland, in 1973

Pyroclastic rocks

Pyroclastic means "fire-broken," an apt name for rocks that consist of rock and lava pieces that were blown apart by exploding gases.

Agglomerate formed close to a vent

VOLCANIC BOMBS
When blobs of lava are thrown out of a volcano, some solidify in the air, landing on the ground as hard "bombs." These two specimens are shaped like footballs, but bombs can be round or irregular in appearance.

Intrusion breccia formed within a vent

MIXED-UP PIECES
The force of an explosion may cause rocks to fragment. As a result, a mixture of angular pieces often fills the central vent or is left close to vents. These fragments form rocks known as agglomerates.

Ash

INSIDE A VOLCANO
Magma flows through a central vent or escapes through side vents. Underground it may form dikes that cut across rock layers, and sills of hardened magma parallel to rock strata.

Vent

Side vent

Magma

Sill

Dike

Bedded tuff (a hardened ash)

WINDBLOWN PARTICLES
Tiny fragments of volcanic ash can travel for thousands of miles in the atmosphere. It forms tuff where it settles and hardens. This ash erupted from Mount St. Helens, Washington, in 1980. The coarse grains were blown three miles (five km) from the crater; the fine particles were carried by the wind for 17 miles (27 km).

Eruption of Mount St. Helens, 1980

Acid lavas

Thick, sticky, acid lavas move slowly and may harden in the volcano's vent, trapping gases. As pressure builds up, these may explode to form pyroclastic rocks.

ERUPTION OF VESUVIUS
The famous eruption in 79 CE produced a *nuée ardente*, a fast-moving cloud filled with magma and ash. The Roman town of Pompeii was destroyed in this event.

Aphthitalite

Aphthitalite

ROCKS FROM GASES
Inactive volcanoes are said to be dormant. Even when volcanoes are dormant or dying, volcanic gases may escape and hot springs form. These colorful rocks were formed in this way at Vesuvius.

FLOATING ROCKS
Pumice is hardened lava froth. Because the froth contains bubbles of gas, the rock is peppered with holes, like a honeycomb. Pumice is the only rock that floats in water. This sample is from the Lipari Islands, Italy.

NATURAL GLASS
Although chemically the same as pumice, obsidian (p. 16) has a totally different glassy texture. Because of its sharp edges, early people used it for tools, arrowheads, and ornaments (p. 29).

CARAMEL-LIKE LAVAS
This light colored, fine-grained rock is called rhyolite. The distinctive bands formed as the thick, sticky lava flowed for short distances.

Basic lavas

These lavas flow smoothly, and may cover vast distances with a thin layer. As a result, the vent does not get choked and gases can escape, so that although there is plenty of lava, few pyroclastic rocks are formed.

RUNNY LAVAS
Basaltic lavas are fast-flowing and spread out quickly to cover vast areas. This specimen of basalt (p. 17) was deposited by the Hualalai Volcano, one of the many volcanoes on Hawaii.

WRINKLED ROCKS
When lava flows, the surface cools and forms a skin that wrinkles as the fluid center keeps on flowing. The resulting rocks are called ropy lavas.

DESTRUCTION OF AKROTIRI
This town on Santorini, Greece, was buried by volcanic ash, c. 1450 BCE.

MULTICOLOURED BASALT
Sparkling points in this basalt include green olivine and black pyroxene crystals.

Sedimentary rocks

Wℋᴇɴ ʀᴏᴄᴋs are weathered and eroded (p. 12) they break down into smaller pieces of rock and minerals. This material, which is called sediment, may eventually be carried to a new site, often in the sea or in riverbeds. The sediments are deposited in layers that become buried and compacted. Over time the particles are bound together to form new rocks, known as sedimentary rocks. In large outcrops it is often possible to see the various layers of sediment with the naked eye.

THIN SECTION OF LIMESTONE
Under the microscope (p. 42), fine details in this ammonite limestone are revealed. The ammonite shells (p. 39) show up clearly against the mud background. Ammonites are now extinct, and we know this rock must be about 160 million years old.

Ammonite shell

Mud background

RAW INGREDIENTS *above*
Foraminifera are marine organisms that discharge lime. They are rarely bigger than a pinhead, but they play an extremely important part in rock building. When they die, the shells fall to the ocean floor, where they eventually become compressed into limestone.

Fossilized shells embedded in rock

Chalk

Oolitic limestone

Shelly limestone

Gastropod limestone

Remains of gastropod shell

Rounded grains known as ooliths

FLINT
A form of silica (p. 42), lumps of flint are often found in limestones, especially chalk. They are gray or black, but the outside may be covered in a white powderlike material. Like obsidian (p. 16), when flint is broken, it has a "conchoidal" fracture (p. 48).

LIMESTONES
Many sedimentary rocks consist of the remains of once living organisms. In some, such as these shelly and gastropod limestones, the remains of animals are clearly visible in the rock. However, chalk, which is also a limestone, is formed from the skeletons of tiny sea animals that are too small to see with the naked eye. Another limestone, oolite, forms in the sea as calcite builds up around grains of sand. When the grains are rolled backward and forward by waves, they become larger.

ALGAL LIMESTONE
So-called "muddy" limestones like this are often referred to as landscape marbles. This is because when the minerals crystallize they may produce patterns in the shape of trees and bushes.

Hole filled, irregular-shaped rock

CALCAREOUS TUFA
This extraordinary looking porous rock is formed by the evaporation of spring water and is sometimes found in limestone caves (p. 22).

EVAPORTTES
Some sedimentary rocks are formed from the evaporation of saline waters. Examples of these include gypsum and halite. Halite is more commonly known as rock salt, from which we get table salt. Gypsum is used to make plaster of Paris, and in its massive form is called alabaster. Both halite and gypsum are minerals that can be found in large deposits worldwide at sites where evaporation of sea water has occurred.

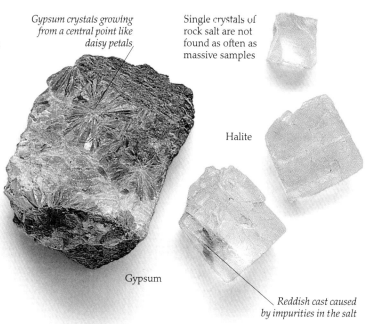

Gypsum crystals growing from a central point like daisy petals

Single crystals of rock salt are not found as often as massive samples

Halite

Gypsum

Reddish cast caused by impurities in the salt

THE GRAND CANYON
This spectacular scenery was formed by the erosion of red sandstone and limestone.

Grit

Red sandstone

SANDSTONES
Both of these rocks are made by the cementing together of grains of sand, but their texture varies. The red sandstone was formed in a desert where the quartz grains were rounded and polished by the wind. The grains in grit are more angular since they were buried quickly, before they could be smoothed by rubbing.

CLAY
Clay is formed by very fine grains that cannot be seen by the naked eye, and feels sticky when wet. It may be gray, black, white, or yellowish. When it is compacted and all the water forced out of it, it forms hard rocks called mudstone or shale.

BEDDED VOLCANIC ASH
In many sedimentary rocks it is possible to distinguish the individual layers of sediments because they form visible bands. Here, the stripes are layers of volcanic ash. The surface has been polished to highlight this feature.

Flint pebble

CONGLOMERATE
The flint pebbles in this rock were rounded by water as they were rolled about at the bottom of rivers or seas. After they were buried, they gradually became cemented together to form a rock known as conglomerate.

Large rock fragment

BRECCIA
Like conglomerate, breccias contain fragments of rock. However, these are much more angular since they have not been rounded by water or carried far from their original home—often the scree (broken rocks) at the bottom of cliffs.

Limestone caves

SPECTACULAR CAVES, lined with dripping stalactites and giant stalagmites are perhaps the best known of limestone wonders. The caves are formed as a result of slightly acidic rainwater turning the carbonate into bicarbonate. This material is soluble in water and is carried away. In addition to caves, this process also produces several other characteristic features, including limestone pavements and karst landscapes.

Top section attached to the roof of cave

Point of intersection

Stalactites of this thickness may take hundreds of years to form

STALACTITES
Stalactites are formed in caves by groundwater containing dissolved lime. The water drips from the roof and leaves a thin deposit as it evaporates. Growing down from the roof, they increase in size by a fraction of an inch each year and may eventually be many yards long. Where the water supply is seasonal, stalactites may show annual growth rings like those of tree trunks.

Single stalactite formed from two smaller ones growing together

Swallow hole through which surface water flows underground

Limestone pavement consisting of large, jointed blocks

Underground lake *Caves*

LIMESTONE LANDSCAPES
Rainwater dissolves calcite in limestone, producing deep, narrow cracks (grikes). Over time, the water percolating down such cracks enlarges them into passages. The surface remains dry, but flowing water dissolves the rock, producing "swallow holes" at the junctions between grikes. Underground streams flow through caves and form subterranean lakes. Some calcite is redeposited in the caves to form stalactites and stalagmites.

TUFA
Tufa is known as a precipitate, (p. 21) and forms when lime is deposited from water onto a rock surface in areas of low rainfall. If a man-made object is left in water with a lot of lime, it may become coated in tufa.

Coral-like structure

PLAN DE SALES, FRANCE
Limestone pavements consist of large, cracked, flat blocks ("clints") of rock. They occur where weathering of pure limestone leaves nothing behind, such as clay, to make soil.

EASE GILL CAVES, ENGLAND
The fine stalactites and stalagmites in this cave form the most spectacular part of a much larger, complex cave system under the hills of the Lancashire Pennines. In fact, this is the largest cave system in Great Britain.

Odd-shaped
stalactite

*Prominent growth rings
mark the gradual
development of the
stalactite as each
deposit formed*

*Point onto which
overhead drips fall*

Orange twin
stalactite

Last section to grow

**STONE FOREST,
CHINA**
The staggering
landscape of the
Hunan Province of
China is typical of
"karst" scenery.
Named after the
limestone area of
Karst in Yugoslavia,
the term is applied
to many limestone
regions, including the
Cumberland Plateau,
United States, parts of
the Blue Mountains,
Australia, and the
Causses, France.

**PAMUKKALE FALLS,
TURKEY**
Beautiful travertine
terraces are formed
from the precipitation
of calcite from hot
springs in limestone
areas. Travertine
is quarried as a
decorative building
stone (p. 27).

STALAGMITES
Stalagmites are
formed on the floor
of caves where
water has dripped
from the roof or a
stalactite above.
Like stalactites,
they develop as
water containing
dissolved lime
evaporates.
Stalactites and
stalagmites can
grow together
and meet to form
pillars. These
have been
described as
"organ pipes,"
"hanging curtains,"
and "portcullises."

*Color caused by
impurities in the deposit*

Layer of relatively pure calcite

*End attached to
floor of the cave*

INSIDE A STALACTITE
This specimen has been sliced through the center to reveal
colored bands. The different colors show how the stalactite
formed from deposits of lime with varying degrees of purity.
The purest parts are the whitest.

Metamorphic rocks

Schist

THESE ROCKS get their name from the Greek words *meta* and *morphe*, meaning "change of form," and are igneous (p. 16) or sedimentary (p. 20) rocks that have been altered by heat and/ or pressure. Such conditions can occur during mountain building processes (p. 6); buried rocks may then be subjected to high temperatures and may be squeezed or folded, causing minerals in the rocks to recrystallize and new minerals to form. Other metamorphic rocks are formed when rocks surrounding a hot igneous mass are "baked" by the heat.

THIN SECTION OF GARNET-MICA SCHIST
Seen through a petrological microscope (p. 42), this Norwegian rock reveals brightly colored, blade-shaped mica crystals. Quartz and feldspar appear as various shades of gray.

Saccharoidal marble

Evenly sized grains give a sugary appearance

MARBLES
When limestone is exposed to very high temperatures, new crystals of calcite grow and form the compact rock known as marble. It is sometimes confused with quartzite, that looks similar. However, marble is softer and may easily be scratched with a knife. Some medium-grained marble looks sugary and is called saccharoidal. This specimen comes from Korea. The marble on the far right was formed from limestone containing impurites, such as pyroxene.

Nodular gray marble

Pyroxene-bearing marble

Chiastolite slate

Spotted hornfels

_____ Elongated chiastolite crystals

_____ Groups of carbon

Spotted slate

FROM SLATE TO HORNFELS
The irregular speckles in spotted slate are small groups of carbon, formed by heat from an igneous intrusion. In rocks nearer the intrusion, the temperature is considerably higher and needlelike crystals of chiastolite form in the slate. The rocks very close to the intrusion become so hot that they completely recrystallize and form a tough new rock called hornfels.

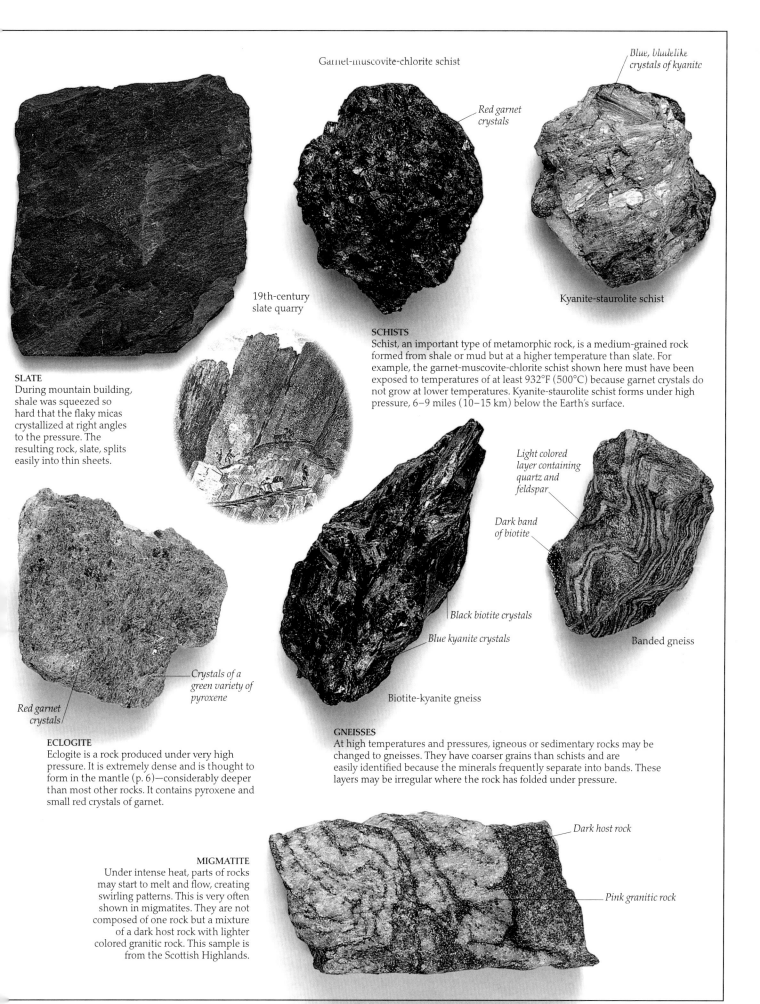

Garnet-muscovite-chlorite schist

Red garnet crystals

Blue, bladelike crystals of kyanite

Kyanite-staurolite schist

19th-century slate quarry

SLATE
During mountain building, shale was squeezed so hard that the flaky micas crystallized at right angles to the pressure. The resulting rock, slate, splits easily into thin sheets.

SCHISTS
Schist, an important type of metamorphic rock, is a medium-grained rock formed from shale or mud but at a higher temperature than slate. For example, the garnet-muscovite-chlorite schist shown here must have been exposed to temperatures of at least 932°F (500°C) because garnet crystals do not grow at lower temperatures. Kyanite-staurolite schist forms under high pressure, 6–9 miles (10–15 km) below the Earth's surface.

Light colored layer containing quartz and feldspar

Dark band of biotite

Banded gneiss

Black biotite crystals

Blue kyanite crystals

Crystals of a green variety of pyroxene

Red garnet crystals

Biotite-kyanite gneiss

ECLOGITE
Eclogite is a rock produced under very high pressure. It is extremely dense and is thought to form in the mantle (p. 6)—considerably deeper than most other rocks. It contains pyroxene and small red crystals of garnet.

GNEISSES
At high temperatures and pressures, igneous or sedimentary rocks may be changed to gneisses. They have coarser grains than schists and are easily identified because the minerals frequently separate into bands. These layers may be irregular where the rock has folded under pressure.

Dark host rock

Pink granitic rock

MIGMATITE
Under intense heat, parts of rocks may start to melt and flow, creating swirling patterns. This is very often shown in migmatites. They are not composed of one rock but a mixture of a dark host rock with lighter colored granitic rock. This sample is from the Scottish Highlands.

Marble

STRICTLY SPEAKING, marble is a metamorphosed limestone (p. 24). However, the term "marble" is often used in the stone industry for a variety of other rocks. All are valued for their attractive range of textures and colors, and because they are easily cut and polished. Marble has been widely used for sculpture, particularly by the ancient Greeks; its use in building reached a peak under the Romans.

IN THE RAW *below*
A true marble, this unpolished, coarsely crystalline specimen of Mijas Marble is from Malaga, Spain. Polishing will give it a smooth surface.

MEDICI MADONNA
Michelangelo sculpted this statue from Carrara marble, c. 1530.

CARRARA QUARRY
The world's most famous marble comes from the Carrara quarry in Tuscany, Italy. Michelangelo used it since it was the local stone.

GREEK CONNECTION
Originally from the Greek Island of Euboea, streaked Cipollino marble (above) is now quarried in Switzerland, the island of Elba, and Vermont. It was used in the Byzantine church of St. Sophia in Istanbul, Turkey.

ITALIAN SPECIALTY *left*
Gray Bardilla marble comes from Carrara, Italy, an area famous for its marble production.

ITALIAN ELEGANCE *right*
Another striking Italian marble is the black and gold variety from Liguria.

TUSCAN STONES
The distinctive texture of
the Italian decorative stone,
Breccia Violetto, was the reason for
its use in the Paris Opera House in 1875.

TAJ MAHAL
India's most famous monument, the Taj
Mahal, is made of assorted marbles.

**SOUTH
AFRICAN SWIRLS**
Polished travertine, a
variety of tufa (pp. 21
and 23) has beautiful
swirling patterns. This
specimen is from Cape
Province, South Africa.

SWISS ORIGINS
The limestone breccia
known as Macchiavecchia
is quarried in
Mendrisio, Switzerland.

Detail of marble
inlay work on
the Taj Mahal

AFRICAN COPPER *left*
The vivid coloring of
Green Verdite is caused
by the presence
of copper.
It comes from
Swaziland, Africa.

ALGERIAN ROCK *bottom*
Breche Sanguine or Red African
is a red breccia (p. 21) from
Algeria. The Romans used it in
the Pantheon, Rome.

The first flint tools

BECAUSE FLINT SPLITS in any direction, fractures to a sharp edge, and is fairly widespread, it was adopted by prehistoric people to fashion sharp tools. In the beginning, these were crude choppers, but gradually more sophisticated weaponry and tools such as scrapers and knives were developed.

Rough flint nodule found in Chalk areas

Flint flakes and chippings

Leather thong securing flint and antler sleeve to handle

TOOLS FROM FLINT
Flint was shaped by detaching flakes from a nodule to leave a core that gradually became more refined.

Sharp edged tool used for skinning and cutting

STONE-ON-STONE
The earliest tools were made by striking a stone against the flint, to remove chips and leave sharp jagged edges.

PRESSURE-FLAKING
More efficient cutting edges and finer chips were achieved with sharp, pointed implements, such as antler bone.

Scrapers were used to dress animal hides during the Neolithic period

Large sharpened hand ax

Cutting edge

Light-colored hand ax

Small sharpened hand ax

Crude early chopper

Rough cutting edge

Prehistoric men using hand axes

HAND AXES
Paleolithic hand axes were used for smashing animal bones, skinning hunted animals, cutting wood, and sometimes even for cutting plants. The well-developed, dark axes are between 70,000 and 300,000 years old. The smaller of the two may once have been larger and been reduced in size by sharpening. The lighter colored ax dates to around 70,000–35,000 BCE.

Sharp cutting edge

Hafted adzes were used to hollow out and shape canoes

Mesolithic adze

Antler sleeve

HAFTED ADZES
Adzes are identified by their asymmetrical cutting edge, and the way they are hafted with the blade at right angles to the handle. They were swung vertically rather than horizontally, and used for shaping wood. These specimens date to the Mesolithic period (10,000–4000 BCE).

Adze mounted directly onto handle

Asymmetrical cutting edge of flint

Reproduction wooden handle

SICKLE
Flint sickles imply the cultivation of crops. The long, slightly curved blade was used to reap crops. Sometimes the sickles have a "gloss" on their cutting edge that is a polish caused by repeated harvesting. This one, mounted in a reproduction handle, is of Neolithic age (4000–2300 BCE).

9th-century obsidian ax from Mexico

Reproduction wooden handle

Spearhead with obsidian blade from the Admiralty Islands, off Papua New Guinea

OBSIDIAN
Like flint, obsidian was fashioned into early tools because it fractures with sharp edges. It was even used as a primitive mirror.

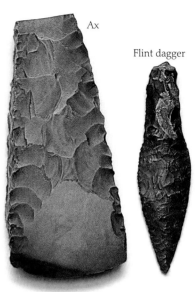

DANISH AX AND DAGGER
This Early Bronze Age ax, found in the Thames River in England, is known to be an imported piece because of its shape. This fact and the careful polish applied to it suggest it was a prestigious object. This is also true of the Early Bronze Age flint dagger (2300–1200 BCE). Its shape imitates the earliest copper daggers, that would initially have been very rare, highly valued items.

Ax

Flint dagger

ARROWHEADS
The bow and arrow was first invented in the Mesolithic period, and it continued to be used for hunting in the Early Neolithic period, when leaf-shaped arrowheads were common. Later, in the Beaker period (2750–1800 BCE), barbed arrowheads became characteristic. It was a time of change with the introduction of metalworking.

Neolithic leaf-shaped arrowheads

Beaker period arrowheads

FLINT DAGGERS
These two daggers are also from the Beaker period. Their rarity, and the care with which they were made, suggest they may have served as both status symbols and weapons.

Rocks as tools

F<small>LINT WAS NOT THE ONLY ROCK</small> utilized by early people. Archeologists have found numerous examples of stone implements from many different cultures around the world. Some were used as weapons, others as agricultural or domestic tools, ranging from mortars (for grinding) to storage vessels and makeup palettes. Many weapons appear never to have been used, and may have been purely status symbols.

Brazilian stone ax

Neolithic ax showing a highly polished surface

Neolithic ax made of diorite, an igneous rock

Neolithic ax made of rhyolitic tuff, a volcanic rock

Reproduction wooden stick

Sharpened wooden point for digging hard ground

South African digging stick with horn point and stone weight

STONE AXES
All these stone axes date from the Neolithic period in Britain (4000–2300 BCE). They are highly polished, and tougher than flaked, flint axes. They must have been traded over long distances as the source rocks were hundreds of miles from the places where the axes were found.

Wedge to stop the stone from moving

Bored quartzite pebble

BATTLE AXES
These perforated (pierced with holes) axes belong to the Early Bronze Age (2300–1200 BCE). The top two could have served as weapons but the bottom one is usually described as an "ax-hammer," because one end could have been used as an ax, the other as a hammer. Because they are preserved so well, they were probably just as much for display as for use.

Carved stone maul—a war club or mace—made by Haida Indians, a North American tribe who live on islands off British Columbia, Canada

Ax end

WEIGHTED DIGGING STICK
Pebbles, like this quartzite example, were sometimes pierced and used to weight the end of pointed wooden sticks. During the Mesolithic and Neolithic periods (10,000–2300 BCE) such sticks were used to break up the ground to plant crops or dig up roots.

Breaking up ground with a digging stick before planting

Side view of battle ax made of diorite

Top view of battle ax

Dual purpose granite ax-hammer

Hammer end

WHETSTONES
Bronze implements were sharpened by rubbing the blunt edge against a long whetstone. Often the stones were perforated so that they could be hung on a loop around the neck or belt. These whetstones are from the Bronze Age (2300–700 BCE).

Engraved Viking forge stone made of soapstone, used in making metal weapons and tools

A bird-shaped mortar carved by Haida Indians (opposite)

MARBLE MAKEUP PALETTE
Roman cosmetics included chalk and powdered lead to whiten the face and arms, red ocher to tint the lips and cheeks, and soot to darken the eyebrows. Using fine bronze or bone spoonlike implements, small amounts were placed on stone palettes and mixed with water or a water-soluble gum. They could then be applied as a paint or paste.

STONE SPINDLE WHORL *right*
The Romans also used stones as spindle whorls. The end of wool or cotton fibers was attached to a bone or wooden spindle weighted with the whorl. As the spindle hung down, its weight and rotating motion helped the twisting of the thread, that was then wound onto the spindle.

Handle

Rotating stone

ROMAN ROTARY QUERN
During Roman times a portable quern (mill) was used for grinding corn in the home. It was made of two stones: the lower one was bedded in the ground or fixed to a bench, and the upper stone, held in position by a spindle, was rotated above it by means of the handle. The grain was fed through the hole in the upper stone; the rotary motion forced it between the grinding surfaces.

Using a stone quern to grind corn during the Iron Age

Conglomerate stone (p. 21) attached to a bench or bedded in the ground

Grain ready for grinding

31

Pigments

W<small>HEN EARLY PEOPLE</small> started to paint their bodies and homes, they did not have to look far for pigments to color paints and dyes. By crushing local colored rocks and mixing the powders with animal fats, they produced a range of colors. Over the centuries, as trading routes expanded, new colors were introduced into the artist's palette. The colors of many toxic pigments are now produced in a laboratory.

Brown clay

Powdered brown clay

Green clay

Powdered green clay

EARTHY HUES
Clays were used extensively by early artists because they were widely available and, being fine-grained, were easy to grind up. They produced mostly dull green and brown colors.

Ocher paint

Umber paint

SHADES OF WHITE
The earliest white pigment was chalk (p. 20), although in some areas kaolin (china clay) was used instead.

Powdered chalk

Chalk white paint

CAVE PAINTING
The earliest known artworks were done by cavemen using a mixture of clays, chalk, earths, and burned wood and bones.

COLOR VARIATION IN A MINERAL
Many minerals are uniformly colored. This is useful for identifying them. Some, however, exhibit a range of colors. For example, tourmaline (p. 55) may occur as black, brown, pink, green, and blue crystals or show a variety of colors in a single crystal.

COLOR CLUES
A useful aid in identification is the color produced when a mineral is finely crushed. The simplest method of achieving this is to scrape the sample gently across an unglazed white tile. Many minerals leave a distinct colored streak which may or may not be the same color as the mineral; others crush to a white powder and leave no visible mark.

Orpiment

Cinnabar

Crocoite

Chalcopyrite

Hematite

Molybdenite

Bison from Grotte de Niaux, France, c. 20,000 BCE

BLACK AS COAL
Still popular with artists today, charcoal was well known to cave painters. They found plentiful supplies in the embers of their fires.

Powdered charcoal

Lamp black paint

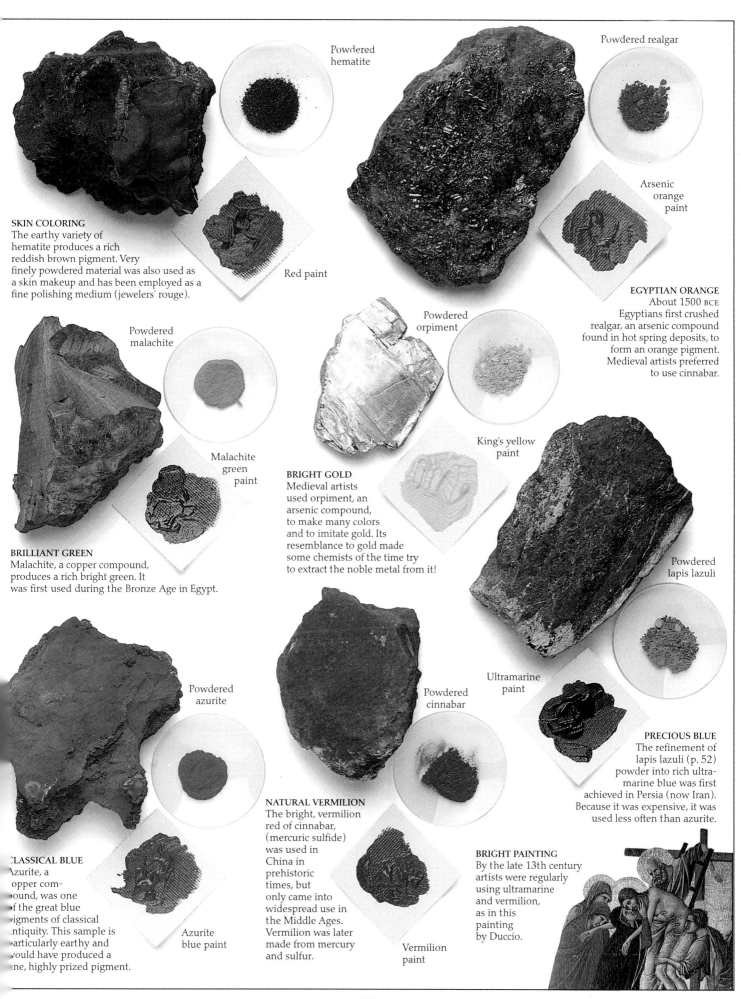

Powdered hematite

SKIN COLORING
The earthy variety of hematite produces a rich reddish brown pigment. Very finely powdered material was also used as a skin makeup and has been employed as a fine polishing medium (jewelers' rouge).

Red paint

Powdered realgar

Arsenic orange paint

EGYPTIAN ORANGE
About 1500 BCE
Egyptians first crushed realgar, an arsenic compound found in hot spring deposits, to form an orange pigment. Medieval artists preferred to use cinnabar.

Powdered malachite

Malachite green paint

BRILLIANT GREEN
Malachite, a copper compound, produces a rich bright green. It was first used during the Bronze Age in Egypt.

Powdered orpiment

King's yellow paint

BRIGHT GOLD
Medieval artists used orpiment, an arsenic compound, to make many colors and to imitate gold. Its resemblance to gold made some chemists of the time try to extract the noble metal from it!

Powdered lapis lazuli

Ultramarine paint

PRECIOUS BLUE
The refinement of lapis lazuli (p. 52) powder into rich ultra-marine blue was first achieved in Persia (now Iran). Because it was expensive, it was used less often than azurite.

Powdered azurite

Azurite blue paint

CLASSICAL BLUE
Azurite, a copper com-pound, was one of the great blue pigments of classical antiquity. This sample is particularly earthy and would have produced a fine, highly prized pigment.

Powdered cinnabar

Vermilion paint

NATURAL VERMILION
The bright, vermilion red of cinnabar, (mercuric sulfide) was used in China in prehistoric times, but only came into widespread use in the Middle Ages. Vermilion was later made from mercury and sulfur.

BRIGHT PAINTING
By the late 13th century artists were regularly using ultramarine and vermilion, as in this painting by Duccio.

Building stones

MOST OF THE GREAT MONUMENTS of the past—the temples and palaces—have survived because they were made from tough, natural stone. Good building stones are relatively easy to work and should be neither too fragile nor prone to splitting and weathering. Today, natural building stones, such as marbles (p. 26), are used mainly as decorative stones, and man-made materials are used for construction.

Quarrying in the early 19th century was still done almost entirely by manual labor

NUMMULITIC LIMESTONE
Nummulite, a type of foraminiferan (p. 20), is one of the most famous limestones and is quarried near Cairo, Egypt. It contains many small fossils and was formed about 40 million years ago. The Pyramids were built with stone from the same quarries.

The Pyramids, Egypt, made of local limestone

Fossils

Tooling

PORTLAND STONE
The surface marks on this English limestone are produced by "tooling," a decorative technique that was popular in the last century. After the Great Fire of London in 1666, Portland Stone was used to rebuild St. Paul's Cathedral.

OOLITIC LIMESTONE
Formed some 160 million years ago, this limestone is used as a building stone and sometimes in the manufacture of cement.

CHRISTIAN MOSAIC
Small fragments of local stones were often used to make intricate mosaic floors.

160-million-year-old limestone used for roofing

Welsh slate

SLATE
Unlike most building materials, roofing stones must split easily into thin sheets. Slate (p. 25) is ideal. However, where it was not available, builders used local, often inferior, stone for roofing.

NOTRE DAME, PARIS
The famous Parisian cathedral was built from local limestone from the St. Jacques region of Paris between 1163 and 1250. Interestingly, the catacombs in Paris are old quarries.

Interlocking roof tile

Pantile

SANDSTONES
Various colored sandstones make excellent building stones. The French town of Carcassonne is mostly built of sandstone, as are many elegant Mogul monuments in India.

Man-made stones

People are now able to manufacture building stone substitutes such as brick and tiles, cement, concrete, and glass. However, all these products originate from rocks of some kind.

ROOFING TILES
In many parts of the world, man-made roofing tiles are molded and fired from clay.

Textured buff brick

230-million-year-old sandstone

GRANITE
Frequently used to cover large buildings, polished granite is also used for headstones. Much of St. Petersburg, Russia, including the imperial palaces, is made of imported granite from Finland.

Red sandstone from Scotland used as a cladding building stone

EMPIRE STATE BUILDING, NEW YORK CITY
This building is mostly made of granite and sandstone, but some man-made materials were used in the construction.

Smooth red brick

GREAT WALL OF CHINA
The 1,500 mile- (2,400 km-) long Great Wall, the largest single construction work on Earth, is built of various materials, depending on the terrain it passes through. Sections include brick, granite, and various local rocks.

BRICKS
Easily molded clays are fired to make bricks. Impurities in clays produce bricks of different colors and strengths, making them suitable for a variety of uses.

CEMENT
This is made by grinding and heating a suitable limestone. When mixed with sand, gravel, and water, it produces concrete, perhaps the most common building medium today.

The story of coal

THE COAL we burn today is millions of years old. It started off as vegetation in the swampy forests that covered parts of Europe, Asia, and North America. As leaves, seeds, and dead branches fell on to the wet forest floor, they began to decay. This soft, decomposing material was later buried. The weight of the layers above gradually squeezed the water out and compressed the plant material into a solid mass of peat and eventually coal. As pressure and heat increased, different types of coal were formed in succession.

Plant roots

FOSSILIZED WOOD
Jet is a hard black material derived from driftwood fragments laid down in the sea. It is very light. Often polished, carved, and made into jewelry or decorative objects, jet has been used since the Bronze Age.

"COAL" AS JEWELRY
A major source of jet is found in Yorkshire, northern England. These Roman pendants were found in York and so were almost certainly made of local material.

OIL SHALE
This sedimentary rock is called oil shale because oil can be extracted from it. It contains an organic substance of plant and animal origin called kerogen. When heated, this gives off a vapor that contains oil.

Leaf

Stalk

Seed case

THE ORIGINS OF COAL
Carboniferous (coal-forming) swamps may have looked like this stylized engraving.

THE RAW INGREDIENTS OF COAL
For coal to form, there must be thick layers of vegetation in areas with poor drainage, such as swamps or bogs. The dead plants become waterlogged, and although they start to rot, they cannot decay completely.

THE PEAT LAYER
Peat is a more compact form of the surface layer of decaying vegetation. Some plant roots and seed cases are still visible. In certain parts of the world, where new peat is forming today, it is cut and dried, then burned as a fuel.

CUTTING PEAT
Like their ancestors, many Irish farmers still collect peat using traditional methods.

BROWN COAL
When peat is compressed, it forms a crumbly brown substance called lignite that still contains recognizable plant remains. Ninety percent of undried peat is water; lignite contains only 50 percent water.

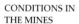

COAL SEAMS
Layers of coal are called seams. They are sandwiched between layers of other material, such as sandstones and mudstones, that were formed by deposits from rivers. These lignite seams are in a French quarry.

"BLACK GOLD"
Under pressure, lignite is converted into bituminous or household coal. It is hard and brittle and has a very high carbon content. It is dirty to handle as it contains a charcoal-like, powdery substance. A lump of coal may have alternating shiny and dull layers, and recognizable plant material, such as spores.

CONDITIONS IN THE MINES
During the Industrial Revolution, many children were forced to work extremely long hours in horrible conditions in underground mines, as this 1842 engraving shows.

MINING FOR COAL
People have been mining coal since the Middle Ages. Some mines are "strip" mines where all the coal is mined at the surface, but most are several hundred yards beneath the land or sea, and a lot of mechanized equipment is used.

THE HARDEST COAL
The highest quality coal is anthracite. This shiny substance is harder than other coals and clean to touch. It is the most valuable of all the coals because it contains the most carbon and produces the most heat and least smoke.

37

Fossils

FOSSILS ARE the evidence of past life preserved in the rocks of the Earth's crust. Fossils are formed when an animal or plant is buried in sediment. Usually the soft parts decay, but the hardest parts remain. This is why most fossils are of the bones or shells of animals, or the leaves or woody parts of plants. In some marine fossils, shells may be replaced by other minerals or an impression of the insides or outsides may be preserved. Fossils are found in sedimentary rocks, especially limestones and shales. Many fossils are of plants and animals now extinct, such as dinosaurs. They reveal details about the animals and plants that existed millions of years ago, and enable paleontologists to date the rocks in which they appear. Fossils showing footprints or burrows, instead of remains, are called "trace fossils."

Muddy rock

Impression of leaf

Beech leaf

LEAF IMPRINT
This preserved leaf is similar to the modern beech leaf. Even though it is about 40 million years old, much of the original detail and texture can still be seen.

Magnolia leaf from Miocene period

Neuropteris—a seed-fern—fossilized in ironstone

PLANT FOSSILS
Many fernlike fossils are found in coal-bearing rocks (p. 36). Formed in the Carboniferous period, they are called "Coal Measures fossils." They are not exactly the same botanical species as the ferns that grow today, but many are extraordinarily similar.

Fern from the Carboniferous period

Fronds of a fern called *Asterotheca* preserved in stone

Present-day fern

Section of a
Nautilus shell

NAUTILUS
The nautilus shell is
divided into chambers.
By regulating the gas in these
chambers, the animal moves up
or down in the water. It swims backward
with its head pointing sideways.

ANCIENT ANCESTORS
This limestone (right) is about 200 million years
old. It is packed with the remains of hundreds of
ammonites. These sea creatures had hard, coiled
shells, and are now extinct. Because the species
changed rapidly and lived in many areas of the
world, they can be used to determine the relative
ages of the rocks in which they occur. The nearest
modern equivalent to the ammonite is the Nautilus,
that lives in the Pacific Ocean.

Ammonite remains

A GRAVEYARD FOR SNAILS
This piece of limestone contains the hard spiral
shells of marine gastropods (snails) from
about 120 million years ago. In places,
the white shell has dissolved, leaving
an impression of the inside.

Impression of interior of shell

Gastropod shell

FOSSIL HUNTING
The abundance of
fossils at the seashore
made collecting a
popular pastime
during the 19th
century.

Garden snails

Rocks from space

EVERY YEAR about 19,000 meteorites, each weighing over 4 oz (100 g), fall to the Earth. Most fall into the sea or on deserts, and only about five are recovered annually. Meteorites are natural objects that survive their fall from space. When they enter the Earth's atmosphere their surfaces melt and are swept away, but the interiors stay cold. As meteorites are slowed down by the atmosphere, the molten surface hardens to form a dark, thin, fusion crust.

PASAMONTE FIREBALL
Photographed by a ranch foreman in New Mexico at 5 A.M., this fireball fell to Earth in March 1933. Meteorites are named after the places where they fall, so this one is called Pasamonte. The fireball had a low angled path some 500 miles (800 km) long. It broke up in the atmosphere, and landed as dozens of meteoritic stones.

METALLIC METEORITE
The Cañon Diablo meteorite collided with the Earth about 20,000 years ago. Unlike the stony meteorite from Barwell, it was an iron meteorite. These are rarer and consist of an iron-nickel alloy containing about 5–12 percent nickel. They once formed parts of small asteroids (opposite) that broke up. The largest meteorite known is the Hoba (Namibia, Africa) that is iron and weighs about 73 tons (66 metric tons). This cut piece of Cañon Diablo has been polished and partly etched with acid to reveal its internal structure.

Fragment of meteorite

Dark, glassy fusion crust formed during passage through Earth's atmosphere

Gray interior consisting mainly of the minerals olivine and pyroxene

EARTH'S CONTEMPORARY *above*
The Barwell meteorite fell at Barwell, Leicestershire, England, on Christmas Eve, 1965. The meteorite is 4.6 billion years old and formed at the same time as the Earth, but in a different part of the solar system. Of every ten meteorites seen to fall, eight are "stones" like Barwell.

METAL AND STONE *below*
Stony-irons form a separate group of meteorites. The surface of this slice of the Thiel Mountains meteorite has been cut and polished to show bright metal enclosing stony material, the mineral olivine. It was found in Antarctica where meteorites have been on Earth for about 300,000 years and for much of this time have been encased in ice.

EXPLOSION CRATER
When the Cañon Diablo meteorite hit Arizona, about 18,200 tons (16,500 metric tons) of meteorite exploded. It created an enormous hole, the Meteor Crater, about ¾ mile (1.2 km) across and nearly 600 ft (180 m) deep. Only 36 tons (33 metric tons) of meteorite remained, scattered as small fragments across the surrounding countryside.

Metal

Stony part containing olivine

HALLEY'S COMET
Water-bearing meteorites may have come from comets, such as Halley's—here depicted in the Bayeux tapestry.

ASTEROID STRUCTURE
Many meteorites come from minor planets, the asteroids. They were never part of a single planet, but circle around the sun between the orbits of Mars and Jupiter. The largest asteroid, Ceres, is 632 miles (1,020 km) across, but most asteroids are less than 60 miles (100 km) in diameter. Their interiors consist of a central core of metal, that is the source for some iron meteorites like Cañon Diablo; a core-mantle region that provides stony-iron meteorites like Thiel Mountains; and a crust that provides stony meteorites like Barwell.

Crust
Mantle
Core-mantle
Core

WATERBEARERS
The Murchison meteorite fell in Australia in 1969. It contains carbon compounds and water from space. Material similar to this is believed to form the nucleus of a comet. The carbon compounds were formed by chemical reactions and not by a living organism. Such meteorites are rare—only about three falls in 100 are of this type.

Rocks from the Moon and Mars

Five meteorites found in Antarctica are known to have come from the Moon because they are like lunar highlands rocks collected by the Apollo missions. Eight other meteorites are thought to have come from Mars.

MARTIAN ORIGIN
The Nakhla stone fell in Egypt in 1911 and is reported to have killed a dog. This stone formed 1.3 billion years ago, much more recently than most meteorites, and probably came from Mars.

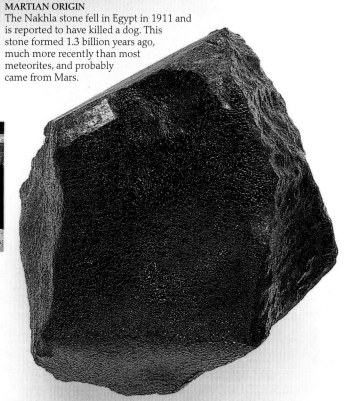

LUNAR DISCOVERIES
The lunar meteorites are made of the same material as the lunar highlands boulder next to Apollo 17 astronaut, Jack Schmitt.

MOON ROCK
The Moon's surface is covered with soil made of tiny rock and mineral fragments. It was formed by repeated bombardment of the surface by meteorites. Material like this on the surface of an asteroid was compacted to form many stony meteorites. Here, the light colored mineral is feldspar, and the darker mineral is pyroxene.

Rock-forming minerals

Petrological microscope

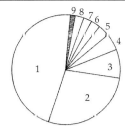

EIGHT ELEMENTS make up nearly 99 percent of the Earth's crust. These elements combine to form naturally occurring minerals. Silicate minerals and silica predominate in most common rocks except limestones. Igneous rocks form the greatest part of the rocky interior of the Earth, and specific rock-forming mineral groups are characteristic of certain types of igneous rocks.

Minerals in granitic rocks

The minerals that form granitic and dioritic rocks include feldspars, quartz, micas, and amphiboles. Feldspars are the most abundant of all minerals, and occur in nearly all types of rock.

Group of black prismatic crystals with calcite

Single hornblende crystal

Hornblende, an amphibole, common in igneous rocks and in metamorphic rocks such as hornblende schists

Tremolite, an amphibole, common in metamorphic rocks

Silvery, radiating, needlelike crystals

AMPHIBOLES
This group of minerals is widely found in igneous and metamorphic rocks. Amphiboles can be distinguished from pyroxenes (opposite) by the characteristic angles between their cleavage planes (p. 48).

SILICA MINERALS
These include quartz, chalcedony (p. 52), and opal (p. 51). Quartz is one of the most widely distributed minerals, occuring in igneous, sedimentary, and metamorphic rocks. It is characteristic of granites, gneisses, and quartzites.

Quartz or rock crystal

THIN SECTION OF A DIORITE
When a slice of diorite about $\frac{1}{1000}$ of an inch thick is viewed under a petrological microscope using a special kind of light (above), it reveals colored amphiboles, plain gray to colorless quartz, and lined gray plagioclase feldspar.

POTASSIC FELDSPARS
Orthoclase is found in many igneous and metamorphic rocks. Microcline (the lower temperature form of orthoclase) is found in granite pegmatites.

Green microcline (or amazonstone) crystal

Twin crystals of white orthoclase

Biotite, a dark, iron-rich mica usually found in igneous rocks, is also a common constituent of schists and gneisses

Muscovite, an aluminum-rich mica, is abundant in schists and gneisses

Silvery brown tabular crystals

MICAS
There are two main types of mica: dark iron- and magnesium-rich mica, and white aluminum-rich mica. All have perfect cleavage (p. 48), splitting into thin flakes.

Minerals in basic rocks

The minerals shown here are all found in basic rocks like basalts and gabbros.

OLIVINE
This silicate of iron and magnesium is typically found in rocks with low levels of silica, such as basalts, gabbros, and peridotites. It often forms as small grains or large, granular masses. Clear crystals are cut as gem peridots (p. 54).

Pink anorthite crystals, a plagioclase feldspar, with augite

Twin crystals of albite, a plagioclase feldspar, with calcite

Green olivine crystals

Crystals of olivine, from Vesuvius (p. 18)

Single crystal of augite

Nepheline, a feldspathoid, with calcite

THIN SECTION OF A BASIC ROCK
A section of olivine basalt viewed through polarized light reveals brightly colored olivine, brown yellow pyroxene, and tiny, lined, gray plagioclase feldspars.

PLAGIOCLASE FELDSPARS *above*
This series of minerals contains varying proportions of sodium and calcium. Plagioclase feldspars are common constituents of igneous rocks.

Crystal of leucite, a feldspathoid, on volcanic rock

Greenish black prismatic crystals of augite, a pyroxene

FELDSPATHOIDS
As their name suggests, these minerals are related to feldspars, but they contain less silica and are typically formed in volcanic lavas that are low in silica.

Prismatic crystal of enstatite with biotite

PYROXENES
The most common pyroxenes are calcium, magnesium, and iron silicates. Augite is a widely distributed pyroxene, and is found abundantly in igneous rocks such as gabbros and basalts. Enstatite, which is less common, is found in gabbros, pyroxenites, and some peridotites.

Other rock-forming minerals

There are two other important groups of rock-forming minerals—carbonates and clays.

Montmorillonite

CARBONATES
These are important constituents of sedimentary (limestones) or metamorphic (marble) rocks. The most common is calcite, the main constituent of limestones.

Illite

Kaolinite (china clay) formed from partly decomposed orthoclase

CLAYS
Clays are an important part of the sedimentary rock sequence. They form from the weathering and alteration of aluminous silicates. Clays include kaolinite, montmorillonite, and illite.

Dolomite, a carbonate, found in some sedimentary deposits usually mixed with layers of limestones

Crystals

THROUGH THE AGES people have been fascinated by the intrinsic beauty of crystals. For centuries it was thought that rock crystal, a variety of quartz, was ice that had frozen so hard it would never thaw. The word "crystal" is from the Greek word *kryos* meaning icy cold. In fact, a crystal is a solid with a regular internal structure. Because of the arrangement of its atoms, a crystal may form smooth external surfaces called faces. Different crystals of the same mineral may develop the same faces but they may not necessarily be the same size or shape. Many crystals have important commercial uses, and some are cut as gemstones (p. 50).

Crystal collecting in the Alps, c. 1870

Light reflecting on the crystal face

Crystals oriented in random growth directions

Parallel striations (lines) formed as the crystal grew

Large twin crystal

Plane of intersection

Well-developed faces

SCULPTED "ICE"
Beautiful groups of natural crystals like this rock crystal look as if they have been artificially cut and polished. This specimen, found in Isère, France, is particularly well-formed consisting of a large twin crystal (opposite) and many simple crystals. The narrow ridges and furrows across some of its faces are called striations. These were formed when two different crystal faces attempted to develop at the same time.

Crystal symmetry

Crystals can be grouped into the seven systems shown below according to their symmetry. This is reflected in certain regular features of the crystal. For example, for every face there may be another on the opposite side of the crystal that is parallel to it and similar in shape and size. However, in most mineral specimens it can be difficult to determine the symmetry because crystals occur in groups and do not have well-developed faces.

SCIENTIFIC MEASUREMENT
A useful feature in identifying crystals is that the angle between corresponding faces of a particular mineral is always the same. Scientists measure this accurately using a contact goniometer.

Reading of angle

Angle between crystal faces being measured

TRICLINIC
Crystals in this system have the least symmetry—as shown by this wedge-shaped axinite crystal from Brazil. Plagioclase feldspars (p. 43) are also triclinic minerals.

CUBIC
Metallic pyrite (p. 59) forms cube-shaped crystals but other cubic mineral forms include octahedra and tetrahedra. Garnet (p. 55) is also classified in this system. Crystals in this system exhibit the highest symmetry.

TETRAGONAL
Dark green vesuvianite crystals, like this Siberian specimen, are grouped with zircon (p. 54) and wulfenite (p. 9) in the tetragonal system.

ORTHORHOMBIC
Common orthorhombic minerals include baryte (from which we get barium for medicinal uses), olivine (p. 43), and topaz (p. 54).

RHOMBOHEDRAL (TRIGONAL)
Smaller secondary crystals have grown on this siderite crystal. Quartz (opposite), corundum (p. 51), tourmaline (p. 55), and calcite (pp. 22 and 48) belong to the same system.

MONOCLINIC
The most common crystal system includes gypsum (from which we make plaster of Paris, (p. 21), azurite (p. 33), and orthoclase (p. 49).

HEXAGONAL
Beryl (p. 50), including this Colombian emerald variety, crystallizes in the hexagonal system, as does apatite (p. 49) and ice. (But each snowflake is different from every other.)

Snowflakes

Twinning

Crystals may grow in groups in cavities in mineral veins. Occasionally they develop in such a way that two (or sometimes more) individual crystals appear to intersect in a symmetrical manner. Related crystals like this are known as twin crystals.

CONTACT TWINS
The mineral cerussite crystallizes in the orthorhombic system. This group of twin crystals was found in Namibia, Africa.

PENETRATION TWINS
Staurolite is also an orthorhombic mineral. In this cross-shaped Brazilian specimen one twin appears to penetrate the other.

Twin gypsum crystals form a distinctive arrow shape from which they get their common name, "swallow-tail."

The growing crystal

No TWO CRYSTALS are exactly alike because the conditions in which they develop vary. They can only grow where there is sufficient space, and if this is restricted, distortions or unusual features may develop. Crystals range in size from microscopic to several yards long. The shape of a crystal or aggregate of crystals make up its "habit."

Coral-like shape

WHITE CORAL
Aragonite, which was named after the Spanish province of Aragon, can sometimes have a "coralloid" habit. This term is used to describe minerals whose shape resembles corals.

Fine crystal "needles"

RADIATING NEEDLES
Very slender, elongated crystals with a needlelike appearance are described as having an "acicular" habit. In this scolecite specimen, gray acicular crystals radiate from the center.

METALLIC "GRAPES"
Some chalcopyrite (p. 59) crystals grow outward from a center and such groups appear as rounded nodules. The habit is "botryoidal," a term strictly meaning like a bunch of grapes.

SPARKLING AGGREGATE *below right*
Hematite (p. 33) occurs in a number of different habits. When it forms lustrous, sparkling crystals it is said to have a "specular" habit, named from the Latin *speculum*, meaning to reflect. The specimen shown here consists of a group of specular crystals.

CRYSTAL COLUMNS
"Prismatic" crystals are much longer in one direction than in the other two. This beryl crystal (p. 50) has six large rectangular prism faces and a flat hexagonal terminal face at each end.

Equant garnet crystals

Mica schist

SOFT STRANDS *left*
These crystals of tremolite are soft and extremely pliable. Tremolite crystals are one of several minerals that have this "fibrous" habit. All of them are commonly known as asbestos.

LAYERED SHEETS
Certain minerals, including mica (p. 42), divide into thin sheets (p. 48). They are said to be "micaceous" or "foliated," meaning leaflike, or "lamellar," meaning thin and platelike.

EQUAL SIDES
Many minerals develop crystals that are essentially equal in all dimensions, and are then said to be "equant." This specimen of garnet (p. 55) in mica schist is an excellent example.

DUAL FORM
Pyrite (p. 59) may crystallize as simple cubes and also as 12 faced solids called pentagonal dodecahedra. If the conditions change during growth, both forms may co-develop, resulting in a series of striations (p. 44) on the crystal faces.

Strongly striated, cubic faces

Sloping dodecahedral faces

Top of glistening pink calcite crystal group

Base of gray calcite crystal group

PARALLEL LINES
During crystal growth, a series of crystals of the same type may grow in the same direction. This calcite group shows a number of tapering pale pink and gray crystals in perfect parallel orientation.

SALT LAKE, CYPRUS
When salt lakes dry up, a thick crust of soluble salts is left.

Stepped faces

DOUBLE DECKER
Chalcopyrite (p. 59) and sphalerite (p. 57) crystals have similar structures. Here, tarnished, brassy metallic chalcopyrite crystals have grown in parallel orientation on brownish black sphalerite crystals.

Sphalerite crystals

Chalcopyrite crystals

STEPPED CRYSTALS
This specimen of halite (p. 21) contains numerous sand grains. It shows excessive growth in two directions along preferred axes, resulting in a stack of cubic crystals forming steps.

Sandy cubes

HOPPER GROWTH
The mineral halite (salt, p. 21) is cubic but crystals sometimes grow faster along the cube edge than in the center of the faces, resulting in the formation of "hopper crystals" that have stepped cavities in each face.

BRANCHING METAL
When space is restricted, such as in confined spaces between two beds of rock, native copper (p. 56) and other minerals may grow in thin sheets. Its characteristic branchlike form is described as dendritic.

"Branches" of copper

Outline of chlorite

PHANTOM GROWTH
The dark areas within this quartz crystal formed when a thin layer of chlorite coated the crystal at an earlier stage of its growth. When the crystal continued to grow, the chlorite became a ghostlike outline.

The properties of minerals

THE MAJORITY OF MINERALS have a regular crystal structure and a definite chemical composition. These determine the physical and chemical properties that are characteristic of each particular mineral, some having considerable scientific and industrial importance. By studying mineral properties such as cleavage, hardness, and specific gravity, geologists can discover how the mineral was formed, and also use them, along with color and habit (p. 46), to identify minerals.

Structure

Some chemically identical minerals exist in more than one structural state. The element carbon, for example, forms two minerals—diamond and graphite. The difference in their properties is caused by different arrangements of carbon atoms.

Carbon atom

Model of graphite structure

Model of diamond structure *Carbon atom*

Model showing how one atom is bonded to four others

Diamonds

GRAPHITE
In graphite, a hexagonal mineral formed under high temperature conditions, each carbon atom is closely linked to three others in the same plane. The structure is built up of widely spaced layers that are only weakly bonded together. Graphite is one of the softest minerals (Mohs' scale 1–2), and its loose bonding enables it to leave marks on paper, hence its use in pencils.

Graphite specimen

DIAMOND
Diamond (p. 50) is a cubic mineral formed under high pressure conditions. Each carbon atom is strongly bonded to four others to form a rigid compact structure. This makes diamond extremely hard (Mohs' scale 10). Because of this, it is used as a cutting tool in industry.

Cleavage

When crystals break, some tend to split along well-defined cleavage planes. These are caused by the carefully ordered arrangement of the atoms in the crystal.

Thin layers

THIN SHEETS
Stibnite, an ore of antimony, shows a perfect sheetlike cleavage due to weak structural bonding between chains of antimony and sulfur atoms.

LEAD STEPS
Galena, the main ore of lead (p. 57), has a perfect cubic cleavage, due to the internal arrangement of lead and sulfur atoms, so that a broken crystal face is made up of many small cubic cleavage steps.

Steps

PERFECT BREAK
Baryte crystals (p. 45) show two perfect cleavages. If this crystal was broken, it would split along these planes of cleavage.

Thin lines show cleavage planes

Smaller crystal growing with larger crystal

PERFECT RHOMB
Any piece of calcite has such a well-developed rhombohedral cleavage that a break in any other direction is virtually impossible.

FRACTURE
Quartz crystals break with a glassy, conchoidal (shell-like) fracture rather than cleaving along any particular plane.

Rounded, conchoidal edges

Hardness

The bonds holding atoms together dictate a mineral's hardness. In 1812, the Austrian mineralogist Friedrich Mohs devised a scale of hardness that is still in use today. He selected ten minerals as standards and arranged them so that any mineral on the scale would scratch only those below it. Everyday objects can be used to test where a mineral fits into the scale. A fingernail has a hardness of 2.5, and a pocketknife is 5.5. Minerals of six and above will scratch glass; glass will scratch apatite and other minerals below it.

GRAPH SHOWING RELATIVE HARDNESS
The intervals between the minerals in Mohs' scale are irregular. Diamond is about 40 times harder than talc, while corundum is only nine times as hard.

1	2	3	4	5	6	7	8	9	10
Talc	Gypsum	Calcite	Fluorite	Apatite	Orthoclase	Quartz	Topaz	Corundum	Diamond

Magnetism

Only two common minerals, magnetite and pyrrhotite (both iron compounds), are strongly magnetic. Some specimens of magnetite called "lodestones" were used as an early form of compass.

NATURAL MAGNET
Magnetite is permanently magnetized and will attract iron filings and other metallic objects such as paper clips.

Clusters of iron filings

Optical properties

As light passes through minerals, many optical effects are produced due to the way the light reacts with atoms in the structure.

DOUBLE IMAGE
Light traveling through a calcite rhomb is split into two rays, making a single daisy stalk appear to the eye as two.

FLUORESCING AUTUNITE
When viewed under ultraviolet light, certain minerals fluoresce.

Specific gravity

Specific gravity is defined as the ratio of the weight of a substance to that of an equal volume of water. Determining the specific gravity may aid identification.

SIZE vs. WEIGHT
The nature of the atoms and the way they are arranged in a mineral determines its specific gravity. These three mineral specimens all weigh the same, but because the atoms in quartz and galena are heavier or more closely packed together than those in mica, the quartz and galena specimens are much smaller.

Mica

Quartz

Galena

Gemstones

GEMSTONES are minerals that occur in nature, and are valued for their beauty and rarity, and because they are hardy enough to survive everyday wear when used to decorate jewelry and other objects. Diamond, emerald, ruby, sapphire, and opal all fit this description. Light reflects and refracts with the minerals to produce the intense colors of ruby and emerald, and the "fire" of diamond. Color, fire, and luster (shine) are usually revealed only by skilled cutting and polishing (p. 60). Gems are commonly weighed by the carat, equal to one fifth of a gram, and not to be confused with the carat used to describe the quality of gold (p. 59).

Beryl

The most important gem varieties—emerald and aquamarine—have been exploited for centuries: Egyptian emerald mines date back to 1650 BCE. Beautifully formed, hexagonal beryl crystals may be found in pegmatites and schists in Brazil, Russia, and many other countries.

Diamond

Diamond is named from the Greek word *adamas* meaning unconquerable, and is the hardest of all known minerals (p. 49). It is famed for its lasting fiery brilliance. The quality of a gem diamond is measured by its color, its clarity, the quality of its cut, and its carat weight—popularly known as "the four C's."

Kimberley mine, South Africa

TREASURES IN GRAVEL
Before 1870, diamonds were found only as crystals or fragments in river gravels, mainly in India or Brazil. In the late 1800s, the discovery first of gravels holding diamonds, and then of kimberlite, made South Africa the leading supplier.

DIAMONDS IN ROCK
Kimberlite is the source rock for most diamonds. It is named after Kimberley in South Africa, where it occurs in a volcanic pipe that has its roots between 100 and 200 miles (160 and 320 km) deep in the Earth's crust.

Diamond crystal

Kimberlite

Cut emerald

EMERALDS
The finest emeralds, such as those in the British Crown Jewels, come from Colombia, where they occur in veins with calcite and pyrite. Flawless emeralds are very rare and most crystals are fractured or contain other minerals. Superficially, these may seem to detract from a stone, but in fact they may be crucial in proving its natural origin.

ROMAN BERYL JEWELRY
The earrings and necklaces contain cut emeralds.

MULTICOLORED DIAMONDS
Diamond ranges from colorless through yellow and brown to pink, green, and blue. Red diamond is very rare. To show the stones to best advantage diamond cutters have, for centuries, shaped table and rose-cut stones and, more recently, brilliant cuts that display the gem's fire and luster (p. 60).

Aquamarine

THE ASSORTED COLORS OF BERYL
Pure beryl is colorless. The gems' colors are due to impurities, such as manganese that produces the pink of morganites. Greenish blue aquamarine crystals are often heat-treated to produce a more intense blue color.

Yellow heliodor

Greenish heliodor

Pink morganite

KOH-I-NOOR DIAMOND
This famous Indian diamond, here worn by Queen Mary of England, was presented to Queen Victoria in 1850.

Corundum

The beauty of ruby and sapphire lies in the richness and intensity of their colors. Both are varieties of the mineral called corundum, that is colorless when pure. Tiny quantities of chromium give rise to the red of ruby, and iron and titanium are responsible for the blues, yellows, and greens of sapphire.

STAR SAPPHIRE
Some stones contain very fine needlelike crystals oriented in three directions. Proper cutting will make star rubies or star sapphires.

SAPPHIRE CRYSTAL
While ruby tends to form in flat crystals, sapphires are generally barrel-shaped or pyramidal. They often have zones of blue to yellow color that are important in choosing which crystals to cut.

RIVER JEWELS
Most sapphires and rubies are taken from gem-rich gravels. The gem minerals are usually harder and more resistant to chemical weathering than their parent rocks and become concentrated in river beds.

GEMSTONES IN JEWELRY
The oldest jewelry comes from ceremonial burials 20,000 years ago. Here, rubies, emeralds, and diamonds decorate a late-16th-century enameled gold pendant.

RUBY CRYSTAL
Known as the Edwardes Ruby, this crystal is of exceptional quality, weighing 162 carats. It is almost certainly from the famous gem deposits of Mogok, Myanmar (Burma).

Cut ruby

Blue sapphire

Pink sapphire

Clear sapphire

GEM SOURCES
Australia is the most abundant source of blue and yellow sapphires; rubies are mined in Myanmar, Thailand, and central Africa. The rich gem gravels of Sri Lanka have supplied exceptional blue and pink sapphires for at least 2,000 years.

Colorless sapphire

Yellow sapphire

Mauve sapphire

Opal

The name opal probably derives from the Sanskrit word *upala*, meaning precious stone. However, the opals used by the Romans in their jewelry did not come from India, but from the Czech Republic. In the 16th century, opal was brought to Europe from Central America and only after 1870 did Australia become the main supplier in the world's opal market.

OPAL MINING IN AUSTRALIA
Apart from its use in jewelry, opal mined today is also used in the manufacture of abrasives and insulation products.

Iridescent black opals

COLOR VARIATIONS IN OPAL
The beautiful blue, green, yellow, and red iridescence in precious opal is caused by the reflection and scattering of light from tiny silica spheres inside the mineral. This is different from the background or "body" color, that may be clear as in water opal, milky as in white opal, or either gray or black as in the most precious form, black opal.

Milky opal

White opal

OPAL'S ROCKY ORIGINS
Most opal forms over long periods of time in sedimentary rocks, as in this sample from Australia. However, in Mexico and the Czech Republic, opal forms in gas cavities in volcanic rocks. It is often cut as cabochons (p. 60), but the veins in sedimentary rocks are usually thin, and slices of these may be glued onto onyx or glass to form doublets. These stones are sometimes made even more valuable by adding a cap of clear quartz to form a triplet.

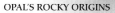

FIRE OPAL
The finest fire opal comes from Mexico and Turkey and is generally cut as faceted stones. It is valued as much for the intensity of its color as for its iridescence.

Decorative stones

TURQUOISE, agate, lapis lazuli, and jade are all gems made up of many crystals. They are valued mainly for their color, which can be evenly distributed as in superior turquoise, or patterned as in an agate cameo. The toughness of jade and agate makes them ideal for delicate carving, while the softer turquoise is used for "protected" settings, for example, pendants or inlay. Lapis lazuli is variable in quality, and precise carving is only possible in high quality material.

Chalcedony

Cornelian, onyx, agate, and chrysoprase are all forms of chalcedony. Pure chalcedony is translucent gray or white and is made up of thin layers of tiny quartz fibers. Chalcedony with noticeable bands is called agate, and the different colors and patterns are caused by impurities.

Chrysoprase cabochon

ANCIENT FAVORITE
Apple green chrysoprase has been used in jewelry since pre-Roman times, commonly as cameos or intaglios in rings and pendants.

Vein of turquoise

Lapis lazuli

Blue lapis lazuli is composed mainly of the minerals lazurite and sodalite, with smaller amounts of white calcite and specks of brassy colored pyrite.

PUREST SAMPLES
The best lapis lazuli is mined in Badakhshan, Afghanistan, where it occurs in veins in white marble.

Turquoise

Found in the earliest jewelry, turquoise is so universally recognized that "turquoise blue" is an accepted term for a pale greenish blue. Its color is largely due to copper and traces of iron. The more iron that is present, the greener (and less valuable) the turquoise.

ANCIENT LAPIS JEWELRY
For centuries, lapis has been used for beads or carvings. It has been known for over 6,000 years and gets its name from the Persian word *Lazhward,* meaning blue.

MESOPOTAMIAN MOSAIC
Lapis was used to decorate the wooden box known as the "Standard of Ur," c. 2500 BCE.

CUT TURQUOISE
The finest sky-blue turquoise occurs in Nishapur, Iran, where it has been mined for about 3,000 years. Another ancient source, known to the Aztecs, is the southwestern United States. Today, this supplies most of the world's turquoise.

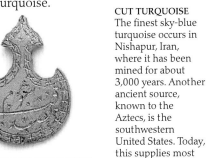

TURQUOISE ORNAMENTS
This object may be of Persian origin. The double-headed serpent (top) is an Aztec necklace. It was sent to Cortez by Montezuma during the 15–16th century.

TRUE BLUE *left*
The vivid blue of this lapis slice is caused by small amounts of sulfur, and has been imitated in glass and in synthetic lapis.

EGYPTIAN AMULET
Many fine pieces of early Egyptian craftsmanship have been recovered from the tombs of the kings.

AGATE
Fine-grained, banded agates form in cavities in volcanic rocks. The most abundant sources of good agate are in Brazil and Uruguay.

POLISHED AGATE
The beautiful patterns shown in polished agate slices were caused by hot, silica-rich solutions filtering through cavities in porous rocks. The microscopic crystals then formed in bands and colored deposits.

CARVED PORTRAIT
Bloodstone cameos were popular in Roman times.

Crystals

Deep colored band

STONE LANDSCAPE
The pattern in moss agate or mocha stone is well shown in this delicate cabochon.

ORNAMENTAL KNIFE
Carnelian is red chalcedony and has been used extensively in decorative jewelry and inlay work throughout history. Here, it has been carved into a knife.

Jade

Originally named from the Spanish *piedra de hijada*, used to describe the green stone carved by the Indians in Central America, jade actually refers to two different substance—jadeite and nephrite.

MOGUL DAGGER
Pale green and gray nephrite was a favorite material of the Mogul craftsmen who fashioned dagger handles, bowls, and personal jewelry, often inlaid with rubies and other gems.

RARE JADE
Jadeite may be white, orange, brown or, rarely, lilac, but the most prized is "imperial jade," a translucent emerald-green variety.

TUTANKHAMUN'S MASK
Lapis, cornelian, obsidian, and quartz are inlaid in gold along with assorted colored glass.

CHINESE ART
The toughness of jade was known to the Chinese more than 2,000 years ago and they used this to make many delicate carvings. These were done in nephrite until Burmese jadeite became available, c. 1750.

NEPHRITE BOULDERS
Nephrite is more common than jadeite and is generally green, gray, or creamy white. Much jade occurs as waterworn boulders. This example of nephrite from New Zealand is typical.

53

Lesser-known gems

IN ADDITION TO the well-known gemstones such as diamond, ruby, sapphire, emerald, and opal, many other minerals have been used for human adornment. Beautiful features like the luster and fire of zircon and demantoid garnet, and the multicolored hues of the tourmaline family, have attracted attention. There is space here only to see some examples of the stones more frequently used in jewelry, but the range of color even in these species is extensive.

Multicolored topaz

Blue topaz

Yellow topaz

TOPAZ
Occuring chiefly in granites and pegmatites, some gem-quality topaz crystals are very large, weighing many pounds. The largest stones are colorless or pale blue, but the most valuable in terms of price per carat are golden-yellow—"imperial topaz"—or pink, both of which are found in Brazil. Pakistan is the only other source of pink topaz but yellow topaz is slightly more common, while colorless topaz is found worldwide.

Blue spinel

Pink spinel

Mauve spinel

Cut spinel

TOPAZ BROOCH
Brown topaz was commonly used in 18th- and 19th-century jewelry. The rarer pink stones were man-made by heating yellow topaz.

SPINEL
Red spinels are very similar to rubies. They were once called balas rubies, probably after Balascia, now Badakhshan in Afghanistan, their supposed source. Valuable red spinels also come from Myanmar, and from Sri Lanka, where there is also a range of pink, lilac, blue, and bluish green stones.

BLACK PRINCE'S RUBY
This famous spinel is the central stone in the British Imperial State Crown.

PERIDOT
This is the transparent gem variety of olivine (p. 43), a mineral common in basaltic lavas and some deep-seated igneous rocks. The proportion of iron in the mineral determines the shade of color—the more valuable golden green and deep green stones contain less iron than those with a brownish tinge. Peridot is softer than quartz and has a distinctive oily luster, and has been used in jewelry since classical times. The original source was the island of Zebirget in the Red Sea, but fine material has since come from Myanmar, Norway, and Arizona.

Vermilion zircon

Pink zircon

Green zircon

Yellow zircon

Blue zircon

ZIRCON
Named from the Arabic word *zargoon*, meaning vermilion or golden colored, stones of these colors, in addition to green and brown varieties, have been used in Indian jewelry for centuries. When transparent stones are cut and polished, they display a luster and fire similar to diamond, but they are softer and chip more easily.

Cut peridots

GARNET

Garnet is a group name for a diverse set of gems that includes almandine and pyrope (red and purplish red), spessartine (orange red), grossular (orange, green, or colorless), and demantoid (green). Fine demantoid has a color rivaling that of emerald, and a fire exceeding that of diamond. Its beauty and rarity command a high price. Almandine and pyrope cabochons, faceted stones, and carvings have been popular for more than 2,000 years. The best spessartines and orange grossulars come from Brazil and Sri Lanka, and the best demantoids from the Ural mountains in Russia.

GARNET EARRINGS
Rose-cut stones (p. 60) make attractive jewelry when set in gold, as shown by these 18th-century earrings.

Rose-cut stone

Gold

Almandine   Hessonite   Pyrope   Demantoid

Grossular garnets

Demantoid garnets

GREEK DIADEM
This section of an enameled Greek diadem, dating from the 2nd century, is inlaid with garnets. Its design is common to many Greek objects of that time.

TOURMALINE
Tourmaline has the greatest range in color of any gemstone, and some single crystals are multicolored. The crystal forms and the electrical properties are different at each end of a crystal. This polarity is sometimes reflected in color differences, especially pink and green. Carvings and cut stones may show this variation to advantage. The best gem-quality tourmaline crystals come from pegmatites. Certain mines in California are famous for their pink and green crystals, and other excellent material is found in the Ural mountains (Russia), Brazil, and Madagascar.

AMETHYST
Purple amethyst is a variety of quartz (p. 44). Colorless, transparent rock crystal is the purest form of quartz, and the colors of amethyst, citrine (yellow quartz), and rose quartz are caused by iron or titanium impurities. The finest crystalline amethyst occurs in gas cavities (geodes) in volcanic rocks in India, Uruguay, and Brazil.

19th-century amethyst necklace

Cut amethyst

Yellowish green tourmaline

Green tourmaline

Blue tourmaline

Pink tourmaline

Brown tourmaline

Mauve gray tourmaline

"Watermelon" tourmaline

Graduating color tourmaline

BYZANTINE RELIC, c. 955
Many Byzantine artifacts were made of gold and decorated with precious stones.

Ore minerals and metals

ORE MINERALS are the source of most useful metals. After the ores are mined, quarried, or dredged (from lakes and rivers), they are crushed and separated, then refined and smelted (fused and melted) to produce metal. Even before 5000 BCE, copper was used to make beads and pins. However, it was the Mesopotamians (ancient Arabs) who first began large-scale smelting and casting. Then, around 3000 BCE, tin was added to copper to produce bronze, a harder metal. Still more important was the production of iron, fairly widespread by 500 BCE. Iron was harder than bronze, and iron ores were much more common.

Bronze ritual food vessel from China, c. 10th century BCE

Bauxite—aluminum ore (p. 13)

LIGHTWEIGHT ALUMINUM
Aluminum is a good conductor of electricity, lightweight, and not easily corroded. It is used in power lines, building and construction, cars and washing machines, pots and pans.

Aluminum foil

Stacks of aluminum ingots

Iron mining, c. 1580

TOUGH IRON
Hematite, the most important iron ore, commonly occurs as "kidney ore"—so-called because of its shape. Iron is tough and hard, yet easy to work. It can be cast, forged, machined, rolled, and alloyed with other metals. It is used extensively in the construction industries. Steel and many household items are made from iron.

Hematite—iron ore

Steel screw

Chalcopyrite—copper ore

Rutile—titanium ore

COLORFUL COPPER
Brassy, yellow chalcopyrite and bluish purple bornite are common copper ores. Massive ores are usually found in isolated deposits that are too expensive to mine. Most copper now comes from large, low-grade deposits. Because it is a good conductor, copper is used in the electricity industry, and because it is malleable (easy to shape and roll), it is good for household water pipes. It is also used in alloys with zinc (brass) and with tin (bronze).

STRONG TITANIUM
Rutile and ilmenite are the principle ores of titanium. Usually found in igneous or metamorphic rocks, these two minerals are concentrated in the weathering process, and form deposits with other minerals, many of which are removed as by-products. Because of its light weight and great strength, titanium is widely used in aircraft frames and engines.

Airliner partially constructed from titanium

Copper plumbing joint

Bornite—copper ore

Sphalerite—
zinc ore

Galvanized
nail

DURABLE NICKEL
Nickel comes from deposits in large layered gabbroic intrusions (p. 17), and from deposits formed by the weathering of basaltic igneous rocks. Small amounts of nickeline occur in silver and uranium deposits where nickel is a by-product. Nickel is used in alloys like stainless steel to help it resist corrosion. High-strength, high-temperature alloys are suitable for aircraft and jet engines.

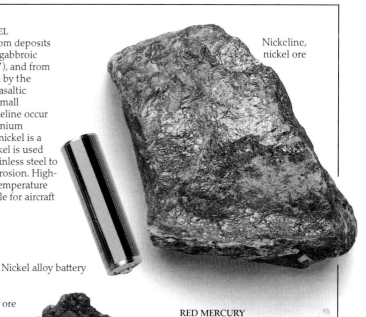

Nickeline,
nickel ore

Nickel alloy battery

BLACK JACK ZINC
Sphalerite or "black jack," as it was commonly known by miners, is the most important zinc ore and is found in deposits in sedimentary and volcanic rocks. Its name comes from the Greek word for "deceptive," since it has sometimes been mistaken for other minerals. Zinc is used mainly in "galvanizing," where sheet steel is coated with a thin layer of zinc to prevent it from rusting.

Zinc processing in
Belgium, c. 1873

Cinnabar, mercury ore

RED MERCURY
The poisonous mercury ore, cinnabar, (p. 33), is found in only a few locations, those in China, Spain, and Italy being the best known. It forms near volcanic rocks and hot springs. Mercury is very dense, has a low melting point, and is liquid at room temperature. It is widely used in the manufacture of drugs, pigments, insecticides, and scientific instruments, as well as dentistry.

Mercury
thermometer

SOFT AND SHINY LEAD
Galena, the main lead ore, is worked chiefly from deposits in limestones, such as those in southern United States. Some lead deposits are only economically viable because of a high silver content. Lead is the densest and softest common metal with a high resistance to corrosion, but it is not very strong. It is used in storage batteries, gasoline, engineering and plumbing, and with tin in solder.

Lead solder

Galena,
lead ore

19th-century Cornish
tin mine, England

Crystalline
cassiterite—tin ore

WORKABLE TIN
The tin ore, cassiterite, is hard, heavy, and resistant to abrasion. Crystalline forms, like this Bolivian specimen, are relatively rare. The modern uses of tin are based on its low melting point, resistance to corrosion, malleability, lack of toxicity, and high electrical conductivity. It is used in solder and tinplate, although aluminum is now more widely used for canning. Pewter is an alloy, with roughly 75 percent tin and 25 percent lead.

Tin can

Precious metals

GOLD AND SILVER were among the carliest metals discovered and were valued for their beauty and rarity. Both were used in coins and bars that were visible items of wealth and were used to buy things. Gold and silver were also used to make jewelry and other objects. Platinum was first reported from Colombia in the mid-18th century but was not widely used in jewelry and coins until this century.

Platinum

Currently more valuable even than gold, platinum's major industrial use is in oil refining and in reducing pollution from car exhausts.

SPERRYLITE CRYSTAL
Platinum is found in a variety of minerals, one of which is sperrylite. This well-formed crystal was found in the Transvaal, South Africa, around 1924. It is the world's largest known crystal of this species.

PLATINUM GRAINS
Most platinum minerals occur as very small grains in nickel deposits. However, platinum-bearing grains are also often recovered from gold workings. These grains are from Rio Pinto, Colombia.

RUSSIAN COINS
Platinum has been used for coins in several countries. During the reign of Nicholas I, the Russians minted platinum coins worth three roubles.

PLATINUM NUGGET
Very rarely, large nuggets of platinum are found. This one, from Nizhni-Tagil in the Urals, weighs 2½ lb (1.1 kg)—impressive, but less than the largest ever recorded, that weighed 22 lb (9.7 kg).

Silver

Silver is less valuable than either gold or platinum, and it tarnishes (discolors) easily. Both sterling and plated silver are made into jewelry and ornaments, and silver is also used in the photographic industry.

MEXICAN ORE-CRUSHER
Early methods of crushing silver ores were primitive but effective.

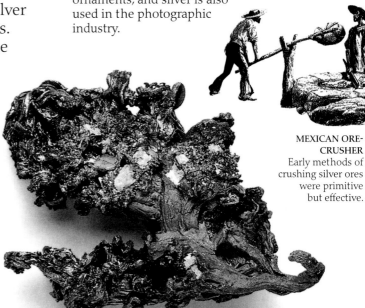

DELICATE SILVER WIRES
Silver is now mostly removed as a by-product from the mining of copper and lead-zinc deposits. In the last century, it was usually mined as native metal. The silver "wires" from the Kongsberg mines in Norway are particularly famous.

CELTIC BROOCH
The Celts fashioned many intricate pieces of jewelry in silver.

SILVER BRANCHES
Occasionally, as in this specimen from Copiapo, Chile, silver occurs in delicate, branchlike, "dendritic" forms (p. 47).

RELIGIOUS BELL
One of a pair, this silver Torah bell was made in Italy in the early 18th century, and was used in Jewish ceremonies.

Gold

Today, this familiar yellow metal is important in jewelry, dentistry, and the electronics industry, yet more than half the gold, mined with so much labor, returns to the earth—buried in bank vaults for investment purposes!

Crystalline chalcopyrite

SOUTH AFRICAN MINE
Traditional gold mining methods required much labor, c. 1900.

THE GREAT GOLD RUSH
During the 19th century, the discovery of gold in both California and Australia, fired the imagination of thousands of prospectors who began panning in earnest.

FOOL'S GOLD
Amateurs sometimes mistake either chalcopyrite or pyrite for gold because of its brassy color, hence the term "fool's gold." Chalcopyrite, the main ore of copper, is greenish yellow compared to gold, and is more brittle and harder, although not as hard as pyrite.

Massive chalcopyrite

VEIN GOLD
Gold may occur in quartz veins and sometimes forms rich encrustations. The gold is removed by crushing the ore and obtaining a concentrate that is then smelted.

PYRITE
Pyrite generally forms cubic crystals and, on a fresh surface, is closer in color to "white gold" or electrum, an alloy of gold and silver, than to pure gold. However, pyrite is much harder than gold.

GOLD GRAINS
Gold is also produced from the rounded grains that occur in some gravel and sand deposits. These deposits are worked either by panning or larger-scale dredging. The gold particles are separated out before smelting.

Crystalline pyrite

Tutankhamun's collar

Massive pyrite

EGYPTIAN CRAFT
The ancient Egyptians were one of the earliest civilizations to master the art of goldsmithing. They used solid, beaten gold. Today, copper and silver are often added to make the gold harder. The gold content is then measured in carats.

Cutting and polishing stones

THE EARLIEST METHOD of fashioning stones was to rub one against another to produce a smooth surface that could then be engraved. Much later, professional craftsmen (lapidaries) became skilled at cutting precious stones to obtain the best optical effect and to maximize the size of the cut stone. In recent years, amateur lapidaries have shaped rounded "pebbles" of various minerals by going back to the process of rubbing stones together, using a rotating drum.

Grinding and polishing agates in a German workshop, c. 1800

Cutting gems

When mined, many gemstones look dull (p. 50). To produce a desirable, sparkling gem, the lapidary must cut and polish it to bring out its natural beauty, bearing in mind the position of any flaws.

THE HARDEST CUT
Rough diamonds are marked with India ink before cutting.

POPULAR CUTS
The first gemstones were cut into relatively simple shapes, such as the table cut, and cabochon cut. Later lapidaries experimented with more complex faceted cuts, such as the step cut for colored stones, and the brilliant for diamond and other colorless stones.

Table cut

Cabochon

Rose cut

Emerald or step cut

Pear brilliant

Round brilliant

Hollow drum

Lid of drum

Belt driven by motor

Rollers

TUMBLING
A tumbling machine is an electrically driven hollow drum mounted on rollers. Mineral fragments are tumbled in the drum with coarse grit and water for about a week. This is repeated with finer grits until the pebbles are rounded and polished.

TUMBLING ACTION
As the drum rotates, pebbles are smoothed and rounded by the grit and each other.

Rough mineral pieces ready for tumbling

Water added with grits

GRITS AND POLISHES
Various grinding grits are used in sequence from the coarsest to the finest, followed by a polishing powder.

Coarse grinding grit used in first tumbling

Fine grinding grit used for second tumbling

Cerium oxide, very fine polishing powder, used at the end to make pebbles smooth and sparkling

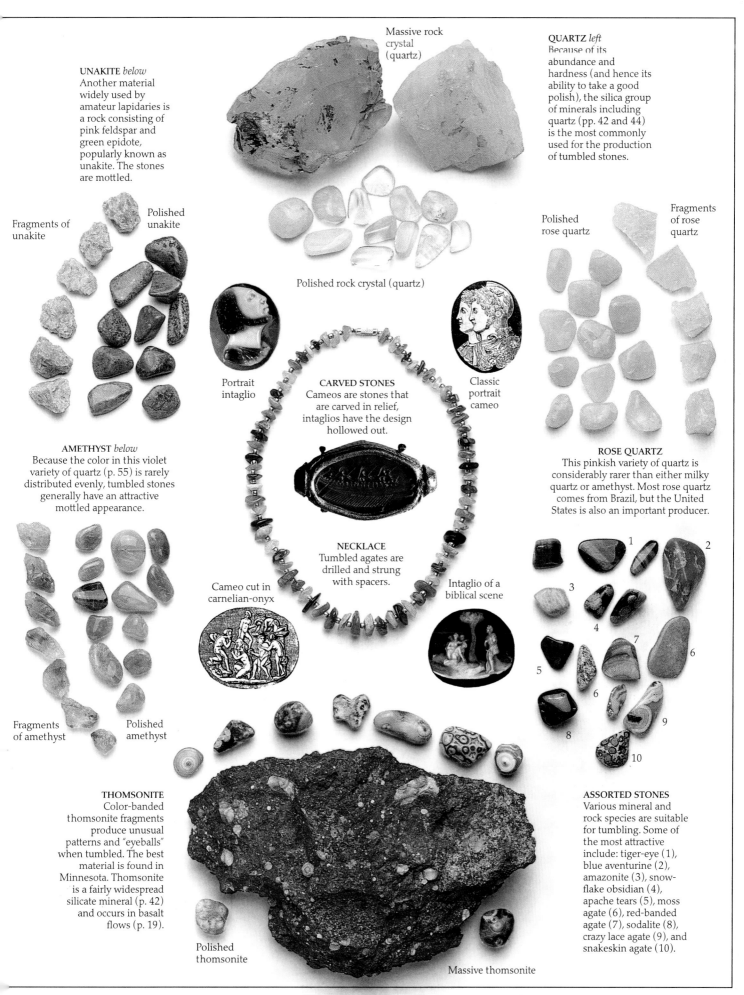

UNAKITE *below*
Another material widely used by amateur lapidaries is a rock consisting of pink feldspar and green epidote, popularly known as unakite. The stones are mottled.

Massive rock crystal (quartz)

QUARTZ *left*
Because of its abundance and hardness (and hence its ability to take a good polish), the silica group of minerals including quartz (pp. 42 and 44) is the most commonly used for the production of tumbled stones.

Fragments of unakite

Polished unakite

Polished rock crystal (quartz)

Polished rose quartz

Fragments of rose quartz

Portrait intaglio

CARVED STONES
Cameos are stones that are carved in relief, intaglios have the design hollowed out.

Classic portrait cameo

AMETHYST *below*
Because the color in this violet variety of quartz (p. 55) is rarely distributed evenly, tumbled stones generally have an attractive mottled appearance.

ROSE QUARTZ
This pinkish variety of quartz is considerably rarer than either milky quartz or amethyst. Most rose quartz comes from Brazil, but the United States is also an important producer.

NECKLACE
Tumbled agates are drilled and strung with spacers.

Cameo cut in carnelian-onyx

Intaglio of a biblical scene

1
2
3
4
5
7
6
6
8
9
10

Fragments of amethyst

Polished amethyst

THOMSONITE
Color-banded thomsonite fragments produce unusual patterns and "eyeballs" when tumbled. The best material is found in Minnesota. Thomsonite is a fairly widespread silicate mineral (p. 42) and occurs in basalt flows (p. 19).

ASSORTED STONES
Various mineral and rock species are suitable for tumbling. Some of the most attractive include: tiger-eye (1), blue aventurine (2), amazonite (3), snow-flake obsidian (4), apache tears (5), moss agate (6), red-banded agate (7), sodalite (8), crazy lace agate (9), and snakeskin agate (10).

Polished thomsonite

Massive thomsonite

Collecting rocks and minerals

THE COLLECTING OF MINERAL and rock specimens and the recording of finds is a rewarding and popular pastime. As a hobby, it is a tradition that dates back to the amateur geologists of the 19th century, many of whom had impressive collections.

COLLECTING TOOLS
The basic equipment required is a geological hammer, weighing between 1 and 2 lb (0.5 and 1 kg), and a range of chisels. Geological hammers usually have a square head and a chisel edge used for splitting rocks. They are specially made for the job; other types of hammer should not be used because they are more likely to splinter.

Club hammer for use with chisels

Geologist's hammer (1 lb/0.5 kg)

Wide-ended chisel

Sharp, pointed chisel

Geologist's trimming hammer

CAREFUL PLANNING
All field work and collecting trips should be planned in advance using geological guide books and maps. Permission must be obtained to visit any area or site on private land. If you are collecting alone, make sure someone knows where you are going. Always carry a compass for help with finding the right direction, and include a grid reference in your field notes.

FIELD WORK
During the 19th century, geologists working in the field developed the techniques of collecting and mapping rocks.

Map

Compass

Guide book

PROTECTIVE CLOTHING
Great care must be taken when hammering rocks to prevent injury from flying rock and metal splinters. Wear protective goggles, a safety helmet, gloves, sturdy shoes or boots, and strong, waterproof clothing.

Safety helmet

Strong gloves

Protective goggles

WARNING
When rock-collecting, there are certain rules you should follow at all times: ask permission before entering private land, avoid disturbing wildlife, wear suitable clothing, use proper equipment, and avoid creating hazards for others.

RECORDING A FIND
The exact location and details of a find should be recorded in a notebook, and the specimen carefully numbered using a pen or adhesive tape. A photograph or sketch of the specimen before collection will provide a permanent field record.

Notebook

Pencil

Pen

IDENTIFICATION
Specimens may be examined in the field with a x10 magnification hand lens. Indoors, a binocular microscope will reveal finer details.

Camera to record site or location of find—when taking photographs try to give some indication of scale

Spatulas for fine work, such as cutting around fossils

Surgical knife for fine preparatory work on fossils

Palette knife for removing small crystals from soft fossils

Sample bag

Newspaper

TRANSPORTING SPECIMENS
Each specimen should be individually wrapped in newspaper or other protective material to prevent chipping or scratching. Crystal groups are usually very fragile and should be packed in tubes or boxes with suitable wrapping and carried in special collecting bags.

Plastic tube

Bubble wrap

Sealable plastic bag

TOOLS FOR FINE WORK
Surplus rock can be removed from a specimen by washing in water and scrubbing lightly with a soft brush. Soft rock such as clay may be dug with a trowel, then sifted for small crystals or rock fragments.

CURATING THE COLLECTION
To avoid damage to specimens, they should be stored in individual trays or boxes within a cabinet of shallow drawers. Some minerals fall apart rapidly in damp conditions, at high temperatures, or under the effects of light, so the needs of each one must be considered when organizing the collection.

Trowel for digging soft rocks

Strainer for sorting material

Paint brushes for cleaning specimens

Cardboard boxes for storing specimens

Labels for documenting specimens

63

Did you know?

AMAZING FACTS

After astronauts returned from the Moon, scientists discovered that the most common type of rock on the Moon is a type of basalt that is also found on Earth.

Spider preserved in amber

The amber we find today formed when resin dripped from trees millions of years ago and then hardened. Sometimes, insects were trapped in the sticky resin before it set and have been preserved to this day.

The deeper down inside the Earth a tunnel goes, the hotter it becomes. The deepest gold mines in South Africa have to be cooled down artificially so that people are able to work in them.

Devil's Tower, Wyoming

Devil's Tower in Wyoming is a huge rock pillar made from lava that crystallized inside the vent of a volcano. Over thousands of years, the softer rock of the volcano itself has worn away.

More than 75 percent of the Earth's crust is made up of silicates: minerals composed of silicon, oxygen, and some metals.

Meteorites found on Antarctica may have come from Mars, and some appear to contain fossilized bacteria.

On some coastlines made up of soft rocks, the sea carves away yards of land every year. Some villages, such as Dunwich in Suffolk, England, have partly vanished into the sea because cliffs collapsed beneath them due to erosion.

Ice has the power to shatter rock. Granite, one of the hardest rocks, can be split by water in cracks that expands as it freezes. The combined weight and movement of a glacier (a river of ice) can hollow out a whole mountainside.

Unaware that it was poisonous, women in ancient Rome used the mineral arsenic as makeup to whiten their skin.

Graphite, the soft mineral used in pencils, is also used in nuclear power plants. Huge graphite rods help to control the speed of nuclear reactions in the reactor core.

Obsidian is a black, volcanic rock that is so shiny that people in ancient times used it as a mirror. The rock also forms such sharp edges when it is broken that it was also used to make cutting tools.

Obsidian

Rocks are constantly changing, usually very, very slowly, due to erosion and forces deep inside the Earth. It has taken millions of years for water and wind to carve out this sandstone arch (right).

Rock arch in Utah

Fossil of *Archaeopteryx*

In 1861, a man split open a block of limestone and discovered the fossil of a birdlike creature with feathers that had lived 150 million years ago. This creature, which scientists called *Archaeopteryx*, may be the link between prehistoric reptiles and the birds of today.

Minerals don't just exist in rocks. Your bones are made of minerals, too!

Q What are the most common rocks in the Earth's crust?

A Volcanic rocks, such as basalt, are the most common rocks in the Earth's crust. Basalt forms from the more fluid type of lava as it cools and hardens. It makes up the ocean floors that cover 68 percent of the Earth's surface.

Q How do we know that dinosaurs existed?

A Dinosaur bones and teeth have been found as fossils in rocks all around the world. In some places, even their footprints and dung have been preserved in rock. It is mostly from fossils that we know about plants and animals that lived on Earth in the past.

Chinese nephrite dragon

Q What is jade, and why does it have more than one name?

A People once thought there was a single green stone called jade. But, in 1863, this rock was found to be two different minerals, now called jadeite and nephrite.

Q Why are the pebbles on a beach so many different colors?

A Pebbles are made up of many different types of rock. Their colors show what kinds of minerals they contain. The pebbles on one beach may have been washed there by the sea from lots of different places.

Fossilized footprint of a dinosaur

Q Why is the sand black on some beaches around the world?

A Sand is made from rocks and pebbles that have been worn down into fine grains. In some places, such as the Canary Islands, Spain, the sand is black because it is made of volcanic ash rich in dark minerals.

Q If pumice is a rock how can it float on water?

A Pumice is hardened lava froth. It is full of tiny air bubbles; the air trapped inside these bubbles makes the pumice light enough to float on water.

Q What made the stripes on the rocks in Utah?

A The desert rocks are made of layers of sandstone. Hot days, cold nights, floods, and storms have worn away the softer layers of rock the fastest, creating stripes in the landscape.

Q What are the oldest rocks on Earth?

A The oldest known rocks came from outer space as meteorites. This piece of chondrite (right) is a meteorite that is about 4.6 billion years old. The first rocks to form on Earth didn't develop until later on, about 4.2 billion years ago.

Chondrite

Q Where do new rocks come from?

A New rocks are forming all the time, on the surface of the Earth and deep in its crust. Some rocks are made from layers of sediment. Others are the result of volcanic activity on the ocean floors and above ground. The Earth constantly recycles rocks by means of heat, pressure, and erosion.

Q What is a desert rose made of and how did it form?

A A desert rose is made of a mineral called gypsum. It formed in a desert when water evaporated quickly. Impurities from the water were left behind and formed crystals shaped like petals.

Desert rose

Record Breakers

MOST VALUABLE METAL
Platinum is currently the most valuable metal, more valuable than gold.

BIGGEST GOLD NUGGET
The largest gold nugget ever found weighed 156¼ lb (70.9 kg)—that's as heavy as a man.

MOST VALUABLE RELIGIOUS ITEM
The Golden Buddha of Bangkok is the most valuable religious item in the world. It is made of over 6 tons (5.5 metric tons) of solid gold.

HARDEST MINERAL
Diamond is the hardest known mineral and cannot be scratched by any other mineral.

BIGGEST STALAGMITE
The biggest stalagmite is in Krasnohorska, Slovakia. It is 105 ft (31.5 m) tall.

BIGGEST ROCK
Uluru (Ayer's Rock) in Australia is the biggest freestanding rock in the world. It is over 2 miles (3.6 km) long.

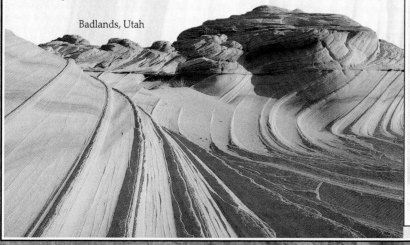

Badlands, Utah

Rock or mineral?

Geologist's tools

GEOLOGISTS CLASSIFY ROCKS according to the way in which they were formed. There are three main types of rock: igneous, metamorphic, and sedimentary rocks. Below you can find out about the main characteristics of each type.

IDENTIFYING ROCKS

IGNEOUS ROCKS
Igneous rocks are made from hot, molten rock from deep within the Earth that has solidified as it has cooled. Like metamorphic rocks, they are made of interlocking crystals of different minerals. The more slowly a rock has cooled and solidified, the larger the crystals that have formed within it.

Large crystals of quartz, feldspar, and mica formed as the rock cooled slowly

Granite

Large crystals that formed as the rock cooled slowly

Gabbro

Dark, fine-grained volcanic rock that formed from lava

Basalt

Glassy volcanic rock that cooled too quickly to form crystals

Obsidian

METAMORPHIC ROCKS
Entirely new metamorphic rocks are formed when sedimentary, igneous, or existing metamorphic rocks undergo a complete transformation as a result of heat and pressure within the Earth's crust. The minerals in a metamorphic rock usually form crystals of a size that reflects the degree of heat they underwent.

Crinkled layers

Folded schist

Fine grain size

Slate

Dark and light bands of color

Gneiss

SEDIMENTARY ROCKS
Sedimentary rocks are usually made from particles that have been weathered and eroded from other rocks. These particles, which range from the size of sand grains to that of boulders, are deposited in layers (strata) and, over time, become rocks. Sedimentary rocks contain fossils.

Large, coarse pebbles cemented together

Conglomerate

Iron oxide gives orange color

Sandstone

Angular fragments of rock held together by a fine, sandy material

Breccia

Formed from the skeletons of microorganisms, chalk has a soft, powdery texture

Chalk

IDENTIFYING MINERALS

No TWO MINERALS ARE the same, and many have a particular color or shape that will help in identifying them. Some form large crystals; others form bubbly masses or grow as crusts on rocks. Below is a sample of minerals and their distinguishing features.

Prismatic beryl crystal

Vitreous, or glassy, luster

QUARTZ
One of the most common minerals, quartz occurs in many rocks and is often found in mineral veins with metal ores. Quartz crystals usually have six sides with a top shaped like a pyramid. Clear, transparent quartz is often called rock crystal and is sometimes mistaken for diamond.

GOLD
Gold is a metal and a rare native element. It is usually found as yellow specks in rocks and often grows with quartz in mineral veins when hot, watery liquids cool. Gold sometimes forms large crystalline nuggets with rounded edges.

BERYL
Beryl forms deep within the Earth's crust and is found mainly in granites and pegmatites. Transparent beryl is hard and rare, making it a valuable gemstone. It has different names, depending on its color. Green emerald and blue green aquamarine are the best-known varieties.

Mass of tabular albite crystals

ALBITE
Albite is an important variety of feldspar, a rock-forming mineral, and is often found in granites, schists, and sandstones. It is usually white or colorless and can also form blocky, platelike, or tabular crystals.

Pearly luster on crystals

COCKSCOMB BARITE
Barite forms in many environments, from hot volcanic springs to mineral veins. Cockscomb barite is made up of rounded masses of soft, platelike crystals.

Sapphire crystals with tourmaline

CORUNDUM
The pure form of corundum is colorless, but it can be found in many colors. Rubies and sapphires are both rare forms and are most commonly found in river gravels. Corundum is extremely hard.

Flat-topped, bright yellow crystal

Orange halite crystals

CALCITE
Calcite is the main mineral in limestone that is usually formed in a marine environment. It is also found in bone and shell, and also forms stalactites and stalagmites.

SULFUR
A native element, sulfur crystallizes around hot springs and volcanic craters. It sometimes forms a powdery crust of small crystals, but large crystals are also common. Pure crystals are always yellow and are soft enough to be cut with a knife.

HALITE
Halite belongs to a range of minerals called evaporites that form when salty water evaporates. It occurs around seas and lakes in dry climates and is best known as rock salt. It is usually found in masses but also forms cube-shaped crystals.

Find out more

YOU CAN GO ROCK AND MINERAL collecting almost anywhere. Rocks are all around you, not just on the ground, but in walls, buildings, and sculptures. The best way to find out more about them is to collect them. There are suggestions on the left for where to start looking. Many museums have extensive rock collections and are a good source of information. Going on a trip or vacation can also provide valuable opportunities to find different rocks and discover new types of landscape. Here you will find suggestions for good places to visit, as well as a list of useful web sites that can provide plenty of additional information.

COLLECTING ROCKS AND MINERALS
Pebble beaches are good places to search for specimens. To start with, look for pebbles in different colors, and see how many types you can find. Other interesting places to look are lakesides and river banks, but always remember to be careful.

Earth Lab

GATHERING INFORMATION
Visit your nearest natural history or geological museum to see collections of rocks and minerals, both rare and common and to find out how the rocks were formed. Many museums have interactive displays and lots of information on volcanoes, earthquakes, and rocks from space.

IDENTIFYING SPECIMENS
You can take your rock samples to some museums for help in identifying them. At the Earth Lab in the Earth Galleries at the Natural History Museum in London, there are over 2,000 specimens of rocks, minerals, and fossils. You can identify your own specimens, examine materials with the Lab microscopes, and consult qualified staff about your finds.

Places to visit

Natural-history museums feature rocks and minerals from around the world, and the experts there can provide information on the origin and composition of the rocks in their collection—or yours. Here are some of the best in the United States:

AMERICAN MUSEUM OF NATURAL HISTORY
New York, New York

NATIONAL MUSEUM OF NATURAL HISTORY
Smithsonian Institution, Washington, D.C.

CALIFORNIA MINING AND MINERAL MUSEUM
Mariposa, California

THE FIELD MUSEUM
Chicago, Illinois

Cardboard trays lined with tissue

Specimen labels

DISPLAYING YOUR COLLECTION
Gently clean your rock samples with water and let them dry, then arrange them in empty matchboxes or small cardboard trays. For delicate items, line the trays with tissue paper. Put a small data card in the base of each tray, with the specimen's name, where you found it, and the date you found it. Group the specimens in a tray or drawer, arranging them by color or by the places where you found them.

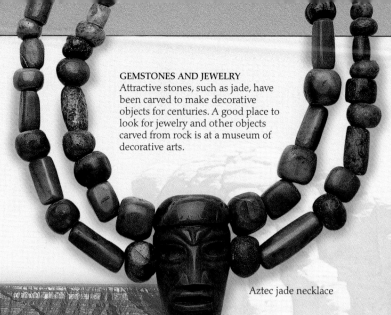

GEMSTONES AND JEWELRY
Attractive stones, such as jade, have been carved to make decorative objects for centuries. A good place to look for jewelry and other objects carved from rock is at a museum of decorative arts.

Aztec jade necklace

HISTORY IN THE ROCKS
Visitors to the Grand Canyon in Arizona have a spectacular view of different layers of the Earth's rocks. The canyon was carved out by the Colorado River and took several million years to form. As the river cut its way downward, it exposed different layers of rock that had been hidden beneath the ground. The rocks are mostly sandstones and limestones and contain bands of fossils from different geological periods. Going down the steep trails to the bottom of the gorge is like traveling back in time through the history of the rocks.

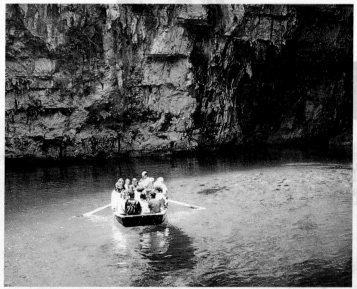

The Grand Canyon

SCULPTURES
The ancient Greeks and Romans used marble to create their finest statues and buildings because it was ideal for carving. Pure marble is white and is smooth and shiny when polished. Look at statues closely to find out whether they are made from marble or another type of stone.

Marble statue of Pieta, St. Patrick's Cathedral, New York City

GIANT'S STEPS
At the Giant's Causeway in Antrim, Northern Ireland, visitors can see extraordinary columns of rock up to 7 ft (2 m) tall stacked closely together. According to legend, giants built it as a stepping-stone pathway across the sea. Geologists, however, say the causeway was made when basalt lava cooled and shrank evenly, forming hexagonal basalt columns.

Cave at Melissani, Cephalonia, Greece

LIMESTONE CAVES AND GROTTOS
Limestone caves are good places to see stalactites that look like giant icicles and brilliant turquoise waters. There are blue grottos at several islands in the Mediterranean, such as Cephalonia in Greece. Famous limestone caves include the Lascaux Caves in France, where you can also see prehistoric cave paintings.

Glossary

ABRASION Erosion caused by water, wind, or ice laden with sediments, and scraping or rubbing against the surface of rocks.

ACICULAR A term used to describe the needlelike form of crystals.

ALLOY A metallic material, such as brass, bronze, or steel, that is a mixture of two different types of metal.

CABOCHON A gemstone cut in which the stone has a smooth domed upper surface without any facets.

CARAT The standard measure of weight for precious stones. One metric carat equals 0.2 g. The term is also used to describe the purity of gold; pure gold is 24 carat.

CLEAVAGE The way in which a crystal splits apart along certain well-defined planes according to its internal structure.

CORE The area of iron and nickel that makes up the center of the Earth. It is about 850 miles (1,370 km) in diameter.

CRUST The thin outer layer of the Earth. It varies in thickness between 4 and 43 miles (7 and 70 km).

CRYSTAL A naturally occurring solid with a regular internal structure and smooth external faces.

CRYSTALLIZE To form crystals.

Group of natural crystals

DEBRIS Scattered broken fragments of material formed by weathering and erosion.

DENDRITIC Having a branchlike form.

DEPOSIT A buildup of sediments.

ELEMENT One of the basic substances from which all matter is made. An element cannot be broken down into a simpler substance.

EROSION The wearing away of rocks on the Earth's surface by gravity, wind, water, and ice.

EVAPORITE Mineral or rock formed as a result of salt or spring water evaporating.

Ground worn away by erosion

EXTRUSIVE ROCK Rock that is formed when magma erupts from the Earth as lava and cools upon reaching the surface.

FACE A surface of a crystal.

FACET One side of a cut gemstone.

FIRE A term used for dispersed light. A gem with strong fire, such as a diamond, is unusually bright.

FOLIATION Sheetlike layers of aligned crystals in metamorphic rocks.

FOSSIL The remains or traces of plants or animals that have been preserved in the Earth's crust. They may be in rock, amber, permafrost, or tar pits. The impressions of delicate leaves, feathers, or skin as well as traces such as footprints are also considered to be fossils.

GALVANIZATION A process by which zinc is added to other metals or alloys to prevent them from rusting.

GEMSTONE Naturally occurring minerals, usually in crystal form, that are valued for their beauty, rarity, and hardness.

Ammonite fossil

Diamond

Sapphire

GEOLOGIST A person who studies rocks and minerals to find out about the structure of the Earth's crust and how it formed.

HABIT The shape and general appearance of a crystal or group of crystals.

HOPPER CRYSTALS Crystals that have regular, stepped cavities in each face.

INTRUSIVE ROCKS Igneous rocks that solidify within the Earth's crust and only appear at the surface once the rocks lying on top of them have eroded away.

IRIDESCENCE A rainbowlike play of colors on the surface of a mineral, similar to that of a film of oil on water.

KARST SCENERY The characteristic broken rock formations of some limestone plateaus.

LAPIDARY A professional craftsman skilled at cutting gemstones to obtain the best optical effect.

LAVA Red-hot, molten rock (magma) from deep within the Earth that erupts on to the surface from volcanoes and other vents.

LUSTER The way in which a mineral shines. It is affected by the way that light is reflected from the surface of the mineral.

MAGMA Molten rock below the surface of the Earth.

MANTLE The layer of the Earth between the core and the crust. It is about 1,800 miles (2,900 km) thick.

MASSIVE A term used to describe a mineral that has no definite shape.

MATRIX A mass of small grains surrounding large grains in a sedimentary rock.

METAMORPHOSE To undergo a change of structure. In rocks, this is usually caused by the action of heat or pressure.

METEORITE An object from outer space, such as a rock, that survives the passage through the atmosphere to reach Earth.

MINERAL A naturally occurring, inorganic solid with certain definite characteristics, such as crystal structure and chemical composition.

Meteorite

MINERAL VEIN A crack in rock filled with minerals deposited from hot fluids.

MOHS' SCALE A scale of hardness from 1 to 10 based on 10 minerals. Minerals of a higher number are able to scratch those of a lower number.

MOLTEN Melted, made into a liquid by great heat, especially with reference to rocks.

NATIVE ELEMENT An element that occurs naturally in a free state and does not form part of a compound.

NODULE A rounded lump of mineral found in sedimentary rock.

OOLITH Small rounded grains in limestones.

OPAQUE Material that does not let light pass through it.

OPTICAL PROPERTIES The various optical effects produced as light passes through minerals. This is one of the properties used to help identify minerals.

ORE A rock or mineral deposit that is rich enough in metal or gemstone for it to be worth extracting.

OUTCROP The whole area that one type of rock covers on a geological map, including the parts covered by soil or buildings.

PALEONTOLOGIST A scientist who studies fossils.

PIGMENT A natural coloring material often used in paints and dyes. Many pigments were originally made by crushing colored rocks and mixing the powders with animal fats.

Azurite, once ground into a prized blue pigment

POROUS Able to absorb water, air, or other fluids.

PORPHYRY An igneous rock containing fairly large crystals set into a finer matrix.

PRECIPITATION A chemical process during which a solid substance, such as lime, is deposited from a solution, such as lime-rich water.

PYROCLASTIC ROCK Pyroclastic means "fire-broken" and describes all the fragments of rock, pumice, and solid lava that may be exploded out of a volcano.

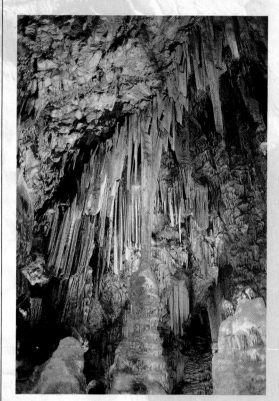

Stalactites hanging from the roof of a cave

RESIN A sticky substance that comes from some plants.

ROCK An aggregate of mineral particles.

SEDIMENT Rock material of various sizes, ranging from boulders to silt, which is the product of weathering and erosion, as well as shell fragments and other organic material.

SMELTING The process by which ore is melted to extract the metal that it contains.

SPECIFIC GRAVITY A property defined by comparing the weight of a mineral with the weight of an equal volume of water.

STALACTITE An irregular, hanging spike made of calcium carbonate (lime) formed as dripping water precipitates lime from the roof of a cave. Over a long period of time, stony stalactites build up in size and may hang many yards from a cave roof.

STALAGMITE A stony spike standing like a tapering post on the base of a limestone cave. Stalagmites form where water has dripped from the roof of the cave or a stalactite above, slowly building up lime deposits.

STREAK The color produced when a mineral is crushed into a fine powder. The color of a streak is used to help identify minerals. It is often a better means of identification than the color of the mineral itself, since it is less variable.

STRIATIONS Parallel scratches, grooves, or lines on a crystal face that develop as the crystal grows.

SWALLOW HOLE A hollow in the ground, especially in limestone, where a surface stream disappears from sight and flows underground.

TRANSLUCENT Material that allows some light to pass through it, but is not clear.

TRANSPARENT Material that allows light to pass through it. It can be seen through.

TUMBLING The process of rolling rough mineral pieces in a tumbling machine with grit and water until the pebbles are rounded and polished.

VEIN A deposit of foreign minerals within a rock fracture or a joint.

Veins of calcite

VESICLE A gas bubble or cavity in lava that is left as a hole after the lava has cooled down and solidified.

VOLCANIC BOMB A blob of lava that is thrown out of a volcano and solidifies before hitting the ground.

VOLCANIC VENT The central passage in a volcano through which magma flows and erupts as lava.

WEATHERING The breaking down of rocks on the Earth's surface. This is mainly a chemical reaction, aided by the presence of water, but it may also be due to processes such as alternate freezing and thawing.

Index

Acknowledgments

Dorling Kindersley would like to thank:
Dr. Wendy Kirk of University College London; the staff of the British Museum (Natural History); Gavin Morgan, Nick Merryman, and Christine Jones at the Museum of London for their advice and invaluable help in providing specimens; Redland Brick Company and Jacobson Hirsch for the loan of equipment; Anne-marie Bulat for her work on the initial stages of the book; David Nixon for design assistance, and Tim Hammond for editorial assistance; Fred Ford and Mike Pilley of Radius Graphics, and Ray Owen and Nick Madren for artwork.

For this edition, the publisher would also like to thank: Dr. Wendy Kirk for assisting with revisions; Claire Bowers, David Ekholm-JAlbum, Sunita Gahir, Joanne Little, Nigel Ritchie, Susan St. Louis, Carey Scott, and Bulent Yusuf for the clip art; David Ball, Neville Graham, Rose Horridge, Joanne Little, and Sue Nicholson for the wall chart; BCP, Laragh Kedwell, Marianne Petrou, and Owen Peyton Jones for checking the digitized files; Margaret Parrish and John Searcy for Americanization.

The publisher would like to thank the following for their kind permission to reproduce their images:

Picture credits
a=above, b=bottom, c=center, f=far, l=left, m=middle, r=right, t=top

Airbus-image exm company: P. Masclet 56bl. Ardea London Ltd.: Francois Gohier 65t. Didier Barrault / Robert Harding Picture Library: 37mr. Bridgeman Art Library / Bonhoms, London: 55mr. Paul Brierley 49b; 51m. British Museum (Natural History): 42m; 43. N. A. Callow / Robert Harding Picture Library: 13b. Bruce Coleman Ltd: Derek Croucher 69br; Jeff Foott 65bl; Natural Selection Inc 64br. G. & P. Corrigan / Robert Harding Picture Library: 23t. GeoScience Features Picture Library: 68tr. Diamond information Centre: 60m. C. M. Dixon / Photoresources: 11b; 14t; 15t; 19b; 32b. Earth Satellite Corporation / Science Photo Library: 7t. Mary Evans Picture Library: 6t; 8; 9m; 12b; 15b; 16tl; 19t; 25; 26b; 28b; 30bl; 31b; 32t; 34t, ml; 36t; 37t, bl; 39b; 40t; 41t; 44tr; 50tr, br; 56mr; 57m; 58tl, tr; 59tl, b; 62t, m. Clive Friend / Woodmansterne Ltd.: 15m, 36b. Jon

Gardey / Robert Harding Picture Library: 40b. Geoscience Features: 18t. Mike Gray / University College London: 17; 20tr; 24tf. Ian Griffiths / Robert Harding Picture Library: 13t. Robert Harding Picture Library: 13m; 18br; 21; 22bl; 23m; 27t, b; 35t, b; 56t; 59m. Brian Hawkes / Robert Harding Picture Library: 12m. Michael Holford: 50tl, bl; 51t; 54t, mr; 55t, ml. Glenn I. Huss: 40m. The Hutchinson Library: 35m; 51b; 56ml. INAH: Michel Zabé 69tr. Yoram Lehmann/ Robert Harding Picture Library: 37ml. Kenneth Lucas / Planet Earth: 39t. Johnson Matthey: 58bl. Museum of London: 28t; 32m; 61tl, br. NASA: 41br. NASA/Robert Harding Picture Library: 6–7, 7b. NASA / Spectrum Colour Library: 11t. National Coal Board: 37br. The Natural History Museum, London: 68cl, 68cr, 71clb. N.H.P.A.: Kevin Schafer 64cl. Walter Rawlings / Robert Harding Picture Library: 26m; 33b. John G. Ross/Robert Harding Picture Library: 53. K. Scholz / ZEFA: 10b. Nicholas Servian / Woodmansterne: 34mr. Silva: 62crb. A. Sorrell / Museum of London: 29t. Science Photo Library: Charles D. Winters: jacket, b. Spectrum Colour Library: 10m. R. F. Symes: 9tr. A. C. Waltham / Robert Harding Picture Library: 22br. Werner Forman Archive: 29b; 30br; 31tl,

ml; 52t, b, 55b; 61m. G. M. Wilkins / Robert Harding Picture Library: 47. Woodmansterne: 58br. ZEFA: 16tr. Zeiss: 41bl. Reproduced with the premission of the Controller of Her Majesty's Stationery Office, Crown copyright: 54ml.

Illustrations: Andrew Macdonald 6m, b; 14ml; 18bl; 22ml; 28mr; 30mr.

Wall chart: All rocks, gems and minerals: DK Images / Natural History Museum, London, UK, except tools (tl), illustration (tr), landscapes (ca & fcra), schist, leaf fossil, slate, pumice, obsidian, chalk, sedimentary rocks, peat, lignite, bituminous & anthracite: DK Images, and Earth: NASA.

Jacket: Front: Gregory Dimijian/Science Photo Library, b; Mary Evans Picture Library, tcr; Natural History Museum, London, UK, tr. Back: Mary Evans Picture Library, ca; Natural History Museum, c, cl, cr.

All other images © Dorling Kindersley.
For further information, see:
www.dkimages.com